FOURTH EDITION

Series Director: **Diane Larsen-Freeman**

Grammar Dimensions

Form • Meaning • Use

Ingrid Wisniewska

Heidi Riggenbach

Virginia Samuda

THOMSON

HEINLE

Australia • Canada • Mexico • Singapore • Spain • United Kingdom • United States

THOMSON

HEINLE

Series Director: Diane Larsen-Freeman
Grammar Dimensions 2A: Form, Meaning, and Use
Ingrid Wisniewska, Heidi Riggenbach, Virginia Samuda

Publisher, Academic ESL: *James W. Brown*
Director of Content Development: *Anita Raducanu*
Director of Product Marketing: *Amy Mabley*
Executive Marketing Manager: *Jim McDonough*
Senior Field Marketing Manager: *Donna Lee Kennedy*
Editorial Assistant: *Katherine Reilly*
Senior Production Editor: *Maryellen Eschmann-Killeen*

Senior Print Buyer: *Mary Beth Hennebury*
Development Editors: *Amy Lawler, Sarah Barnicle*
Production Project Manager: *Chrystie Hopkins*
Production Services: *Pre-Press Company, Inc.*
Interior Designer: *Lori Stuart*
Cover Designer: *Studio Montage*
Printer: *R.R. Donnelley*

Cover Image: © Rubberball Productions/Getty/RF

For permission to use material from this text or product, submit a request online at http://www.thomsonrights.com

Any additional questions about permissions can be submitted by email to thomsonrights@thomson.com

ISBN 10: 1-4240-0338-5
ISBN 13: 978-1-4240-0338-9

International Student Edition
ISBN 10: 1-4240-0836-0
ISBN 13: 978-1-4240-0836-0

My Name is Patricia.
I'm From Venezuela.
I have studied Englis × 3 month.
Becouse is the way to know de lenguage.

CONTENTS

Unit 1 — Simple Present   1

Unit 2 — Present Progressive and Simple Present   18

Unit 3 — Talking About the Future   34

A Word from Diane Larsen-Freeman, Series Editor

Before *Grammar Dimensions* was published, teachers would ask me, "What is the role of grammar in a communicative approach?" These teachers recognized the importance of teaching grammar, but they associated grammar with form and communication with meaning, and thus could not see how the two easily fit together. *Grammar Dimensions* was created to help teachers and students appreciate the fact that grammar is not just about form. While grammar does indeed involve form, in order to communicate, language users also need to know the meaning of the forms and when to use them appropriately. In fact, it is sometimes not the form, but the *meaning* or *appropriate use* of a grammatical structure that represents the greatest long-term learning challenge for students. For instance, learning when it is appropriate to use the present perfect tense instead of the past tense, or being able to use two-word or phrasal verbs meaningfully, represent formidable challenges for English language learners.

The three dimensions of *form*, *meaning*, and *use* can be depicted in a pie chart with their interrelationship illustrated by the three arrows:

How is the grammar structure formed? (accuracy)

form

What does the grammar structure mean? (meaning)

meaning

Helping students learn to use grammatical structures accurately, meaningfully, and appropriately is the fundamental goal of *Grammar Dimensions.* It is consistent with the goal of helping students to communicate meaningfully in English, and one that recognizes the undeniable interdependence of grammar and communication.

use

When or why is the grammar structure used? (appropriateness)

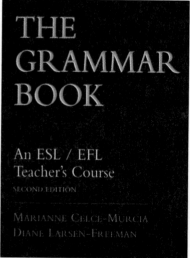

THE GRAMMAR BOOK

An ESL / EFL Teacher's Course

SECOND EDITION

MARIANNE CELCE-MURCIA
DIANE LARSEN-FREEMAN

To learn more about form, meaning, and use, read *The Grammar Book: An ESL/EFL Teacher's Course,* Second Edition, by Marianne Celce-Murcia and Diane Larsen-Freeman. ISBN: 0-8384-4725-2. Enjoy the Fourth Edition!

Welcome to *Grammar Dimensions*, Fourth Edition!

The **clearest**, most **comprehensive** and **communicative** grammar series available! The fourth edition of *Grammar Dimensions* is more **user-friendly** and makes teaching grammar more **effective** than ever.

GRAMMAR DIMENSIONS IS COMPREHENSIVE AND CLEAR.

Grammar Dimensions systematically addresses the three dimensions of language—form, meaning, and use—through clear and comprehensive grammar explanations and extensive practice exercises. Each unit methodically focuses on each students' dimension and then integrates what they have learned in end-of-unit activities. In addition, grammatical structures are recycled throughout the series allowing students to practice and build upon their existing knowledge.

GRAMMAR DIMENSIONS IS COMMUNICATIVE.

Grammar Dimensions includes a large variety of lively communicative and personalized activities throughout each unit, eliciting self-expression and personalized practice. Interactive activities at the start of each unit serve as diagnostic tools directing student learning towards the most challenging dimensions of language structure. Integrated activities at the end of each unit include reading, writing, listening, and speaking activities allowing students to practice grammar and communication in tandem. New research activities encourage students to use authentic Internet resources and to reflect on their own learning.

GRAMMAR DIMENSIONS IS USER-FRIENDLY AND FLEXIBLE.

Grammar Dimensions has been designed to be flexible. Instructors can use the units in order or as set by their curriculum. Exercises can be used in order or as needed by the students. In addition, a tight integration between the Student Book, the Workbook, and the Lesson Planner makes teaching easier and makes the series more user-friendly.

GRAMMAR DIMENSIONS IS EFFECTIVE.

Students who learn the form, meaning, and use of each grammar structure will be able to communicate more accurately, meaningfully, and appropriately.

New to the Fourth Edition

- **NEW and revised grammar explanations** and examples help students and teachers easily understand and comprehend each language structure.

- **NEW and revised grammar charts and exercises** provide a wealth of opportunities for students to practice and master their new language.

- **NEW thematically and grammatically related Internet and *InfoTrac® College Edition* activities** in every unit of books 2, 3, and 4 develop student research using current technologies.

- **NEW Reflection activities** encourage students to create personal language goals and to develop learning strategies.

- **NEW design, art, and photos** make each activity and exercise more engaging.

- **NEW Lesson Planners** assist both beginning and experienced teachers in giving their students the practice and skills they need to communicate accurately, meaningfully, and appropriately. All activities and exercises in the Lesson Planner are organized into step-by-step lessons so that no instructor feel overwhelmed.

SEQUENCING OF *GRAMMAR DIMENSIONS*

In *Grammar Dimensions* students progress from the sentence level to the discourse level, and learn to communicate appropriately at all levels.

Grammar Dimensions Book 1   *Grammar Dimensions* Book 2   *Grammar Dimensions* Book 3   *Grammar Dimensions* Book 4

Sentence level   Discourse level

	Book 1	Book 2	Book 3	Book 4
Level	High-beginning	Intermediate	High-Intermediate	Advanced
Grammar level	Sentence and sub-sentence level	Sentence and sub-sentence level	Discourse level	Discourse level
Primary language and communication focus	Semantic notions such as *time* and *place*	Social functions, such as *making requests* and *seeking* permission	Cohesion and coherence at the discourse level	Academic and technical discourse
Major skill focus	Listening and speaking	Listening and speaking	Reading and writing	Reading and writing

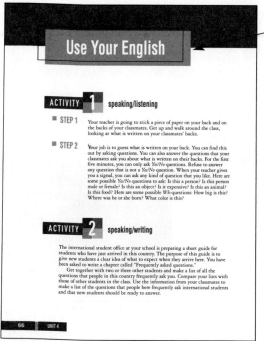

"Use Your English" (fondly known as the purple pages) offer communicative activities that **integrate grammar with reading, writing, listening, and speaking skills.** Communicative activities consolidate grammar instruction with enjoyable and meaningful tasks.

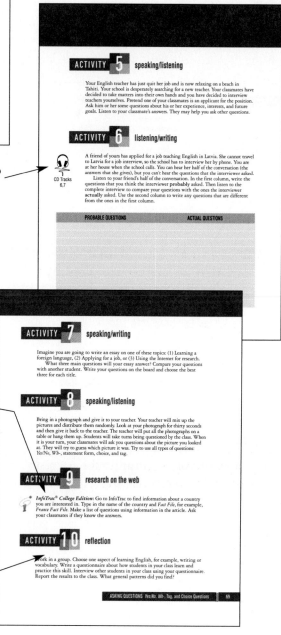

Engaging listening activities on audio cassette and audio CD further reinforce the target structure.

Research activity using *InfoTrac*®*College Edition* and the Internet encourages students to read articles on carefully selected topics and use this information to reflect on a theme or on information studied in each unit. *InfoTrac*® *College Edition*, an Online Research and Learning Center, appears in Grammar Dimensions 2, 3, and 4 and offers over 20 million full-text articles from nearly 6,000 scholarly and popular periodicals. Articles cover a broad spectrum of disciplines and topics— ideal for every type of researcher. Instructors and students can gain access to the online database 24/7 on any computer with Internet access.

Reflection activities help students understand their learning style and create learning strategies.

Guided Tour of *Grammar Dimensions*

Unit goals **provide a roadmap** for the grammar points students will work on.

"**Opening Task**" can be used as a **diagnostic warm-up** exercise to explore students' knowledge of each structure.

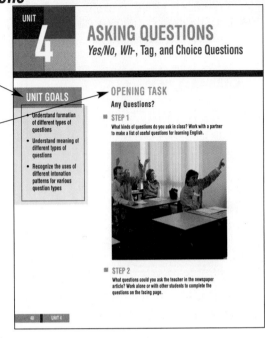

"Focus" sections present the **form, meaning, and/or use** of a particular structure helping students develop the skill of "**grammaring**"—the ability to use structures accurately, meaningfully, and appropriately.

Clear grammar charts present rules and explanation preceded by examples, so teachers can have students work inductively to try to discover the rule on their own.

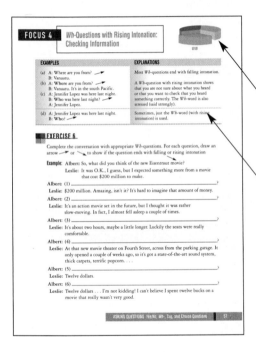

Purposeful exercises provide a wealth of opportunity for students to practice and personalize the grammar.

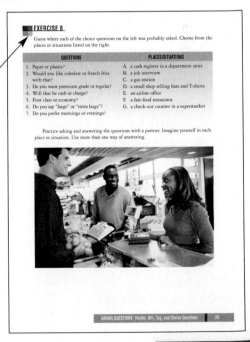

Supplements

These additional components help teachers teach and student learn to use English grammar structures accurately.

The Lesson Planner

The lesson planner facilitates teaching by providing detailed lesson plans and examples, answer keys to the Student Book and Workbook, references to all of the components, and the tapescript for the audiocassette activities. The Lesson Planner minimizes teacher preparation time by providing:

- Summary of main grammar points for the teacher
- Information for the teacher on typical student errors
- Step-by-step guidelines for every focus box, exercise, and activity
- Suggested correlations between exercises and activities in the Use Your English pages
- Suggested timing for each exercise and each lesson
- Lead-in suggestions and examples for focus boxes
- Suggestions for expansion work follow most exercises
- Balance of cognitive and communicative activities
- Explanation for the teacher of the purpose of each activity, in order to differentiate cognitive from communicative emphasis
- Occasional methodology notes to anticipate possible procedural problems.

ExamView Assessment CD-ROM with ExamView Pro Test Generator

The Assessment CD-ROM allows instructors to **create customized quizzes and tests** quickly and easily from a test bank of questions. Monitoring student understanding and progress has never been easier! The answer key appears with instructor copies of each quiz or test created.

Audio Program

Audio cassettes and CDs **provide listening activities for** each unit so students can practice listening to **grammar structures.**

Workbook

Workbooks **provide additional exercises** for each grammar point presented in the student text. Also offers editing practice and questions types found on many language exams.

Web site

Features additional grammar practice activities: elt.thomson.com/grammardimensions.

Empirical and Experiential Support for the *Grammar Dimensions* Approach

Opening Task Activities

The approach to teaching grammar used in the *Grammar Dimensions* series is well-grounded empirically and experientially. The Opening Task in each unit situates the learning challenge and allows students to participate in and learn from activity right from the beginning (Greeno 2006). In addition, students don't enter the classroom as empty vessels, waiting to be filled (Sawyer 2006). By observing how students perform on the Opening Task, teachers can analyze for themselves what students know and are able to do and what they don't know or are not able to do. Teachers can thus select from each unit what is necessary for students to build on from what they already bring with them.

Consciousness-Raising Exercises and Focus Boxes

Many of the exercises in *Grammar Dimensions* are of the consciousness-raising sort, where students are invited to make observations about some aspect of the target structure. This type of activity promotes students' noticing (Schmidt 1990), an important step in acquiring the grammar structure. The Focus Boxes further encourage this noticing, this time very explicitly. Explicit formulations of the sort found in the Focus Boxes can lead to implicit acquisition with practice (DeKeyser 1998). Moreover, certain learners (those with analytic learning styles) benefit greatly from explicit treatment of grammar structures (Larsen-Freeman and Long 1991).

Productive Practice and Communicative Activities

However, noticing by itself is insufficient. In order to be able to use the grammar structure, students need productive practice (Gatbonton and Segalowitz 1988; Larsen-Freeman 2003). Therefore, many of the exercises in *Grammar Dimensions* are of the output practice sort. Furthermore, each unit ends with communicative activities, where attention to the grammar is once again implicit, but where students can use the grammar structure in "psychologically authentic" or meaningful ways. Psychological authenticity is very important in order for students to be able to transfer what they know to new situations so that they can use it for their own purposes (Blaxton 1989) and so they are not left to contend with the "inert knowledge problem," (Whitehead 1929) where they know about the grammar, but can't use it.

The Three Dimensions of Grammar: Form, Meaning, and Use

Finally, applied linguistics research (Celce-Murcia and Larsen-Freeman 1999) supports the fundamental premise underlying *Grammar Dimensions:* that knowing a grammar structure means being able to use it accurately, meaningfully, and appropriately. Form focus or meaning focus by itself is insufficient (Larsen-Freeman 2001); all three dimensions—form, meaning, and use—need to be learned.

References

Blaxton, T. (1989). Investigating dissociations among memory measures: Support for a transfer-appropriate processing framework. *Journal of Experimental Psychology: Learning, Memory, and Cognition 15 (4):* 657-668.

Celce-Murcia, M. and D. Larsen-Freeman. (1999). *The grammar bbook: An ESL/EFL teacher's course.* Second Edition. Boston: Heinle & Heinle.

De Keyser, R. (1998). Beyond focus on form: Cognitive perspectives on learning and practicing second language grammar. n C. Doughty and J. Williams (eds.), *Focus on Classroom Second Language Acquisition.* Cambridge: Cambridge University Press, 42–63.

Gatbonton, E. and N. Segalowitz. (1988). Creative automatization: Principles for promoting fluency within a communicative framework. *TESOL Quarterly 22 (3):* 473–492.

Greeno, J. (2006). Learning in activity. In R. K. Sawyer (ed.), *The Cambridge handbook of learning sciences.* Cambridge: Cambridge University Press, 79–96.

Larsen-Freeman, D. (2001). Teaching grammar. In M. Celce-Murcia (ed.), *Teaching English as a Second or Foreign Language.* Third edition. Boston: Heinle & Heinle, 251–266.

Larsen-Freeman, D. (2003). *Teaching language: From grammar to grammaring.* Boston: Heinle & Heinle.

Larsen-Freeman, D. and M. Long. (1991). *An introduction to second language qcquisition research.* London: Longman.

Sawyer, R. K. (2006). Introduction: The new science of learning. In R. K. Sawyer (ed.), *The Cambridge handbook of learning sciences.* Cambridge: Cambridge University Press, 1–16.

Schmidt, R. (1990). The role of consciousness in second language learning. *Applied Linguistics 11 (2),* 129–158.

Whitehead, A. N. 1929. *The aims of education.* New York: MacMillan.

Acknowledgments from the Series Director

This fourth edition would not have come about if it had not been for the enthusiastic response of teachers and students using all the previous editions. I am very grateful for the reception *Grammar Dimensions* has been given.

I am also grateful for all the authors' efforts. To be a teacher, and at the same time a writer, is a difficult balance to achieve . . . so is being an innovative creator of materials, and yet, a team player. They have met these challenges exceedingly well in my opinion. Then, too, the Thomson Heinle team has been impressive. I am grateful for the leadership exercised by Jim Brown and Sherrise Roehr. I also appreciate all the support from Anita Raducanu, Amy Mabley, Sarah Barnicle, Laura Needham, Chrystie Hopkins, Mary Beth Hennebury, and Abigail Greshik of Pre-Press Company. Deserving special mention are Amy Lawler and Yeny Kim, who never lost the vision while they attended to the detail with good humor and professionalism.

I have also benefited from the counsel of Marianne Celce-Murcia, consultant for the first edition of this project, and my friend. Finally, I wish to thank my family members, Elliott, Brent, and Gavin, for not once asking the (negative yes-no) question that must have occurred to them countless times: "Haven't you finished yet?" As we all have discovered, this project has a life of its own and is never really finished! And, for this, I am exceedingly grateful. Happy Grammaring all!

A Special Thanks

The series director, authors, and publisher would like to thank the following reviewers whose experienced observations and thoughtful suggestions have assisted us in creating and revising *Grammar Dimensions*.

Michelle Alvarez
University of Miami
Coral Gables, Florida

Edina Pingleton Bagley
Nassau Community College
Garden City, New York

Jane Berger
Solano Community College,
California

Mary Bottega
San Jose State University

Mary Brooks
Eastern Washington University

Christina Broucqsault
California State Polytechnic
University

José Carmona
Hudson Community College

Susan Carnell
University of Texas at Arlington

Susana Christie
San Diego State University

Diana Christopher
Georgetown University

Gwendolyn Cooper
Rutgers University

Julia Correia
Henderson State University
Arkadelphia, Arkansas

Sue Cozzarelli
EF International, San Diego

Catherine Crystal
Laney College, California

Kevin Ccross
University of San Francisco

Julie Damron
Interlink at Valparaiso
University, Indiana

Glen Deckert
Eastern Michigan University

Eric Dwyer
University of Texas at Austin

Nikki Ellman
Laney College
Oakland, California

Ann Eubank
Jefferson Community College

Alice Fine
UCLA Extension

Alicia Going
The English Language Study
Center, Oregon

Molly Gould
University of Delaware

Maren M. Hargis
San Diego Mesa College

Penny Harrold
Universidad de Monterrey
Monterrey, Mexico

Robin Hendrickson
Riverside City College
Riverside, California

Mary Herbert
University of California, Davis
Extension

Jane Hilbert
ELS Language Center,
Florida International
University

Eli Hinkel
Xavier University

Kathy Hitchcox
International English
Institute, Fresno

Abeer Hubi
Altarbia Alislamia Schools
Riyadh, Saudi Arabia

Joyce Hutchings
Georgetown University

Heather Jeddy
Northern Virginia
Community College

Judi Keen
University of California,
Davis, and *Sacramento*
City College

Karli Kelber
American Language Institute,
New York University

Anne Kornfield
LaGuardia Community
College

Kay Longmire
Interlink at Valparaiso
University, Indiana

Robin Longshaw
Rhode Island School of Design

Robert Ludwiczak
Texas A&M University
College Station, Texas

Bernadette McGlynn
ELS Language Center, St.
Joseph's University

Billy McGowan
Aspect International, Boston

Margaret Mehran
Queens College

Richard Moore
University of Washington

Karen Moreno
Teikyo Post University,
Connecticut

Gino Muzzetti
Santa Rosa Junior College,
California

Mary Nance-Tager
LaGuardia Community
College, City University of
New York

So Nguyen
Orange Coast College
Costa Mesa, California

Karen O'Neill
San Jose State University

Mary O'Neal
Northern Virginia
Community College

Nancy Pagliara
Northern Virginia
Community College

Keith Pharis
Southern Illinois University

Amy Parker
ELS Language Center, San
Francisco

Margene Petersen
ELS Language Center,
Philadelphia

Nancy Pfingstag
University of North
Carolina, Charlotte

Sally Prieto
Grand Rapids Community
College

India Plough
Michigan State University

Mostafa Rahbar
University of Tennessee at
Knoxville

Dudley Reynolds
Indiana University

Dzidra Rodins
DePaul University
Chicago, Illinois

Ann Salzman
University of Illinois at
Urbana-Champaign

Jennifer Schmidt
San Francisco State
University

Cynthia Schuemann
Miami-Dade Community
College

Jennifer Schultz
Golden Gate University,
California

Mary Beth Selbo
Wright College, City Colleges
of Chicago

Mary Selseleh
American River College
Sacramento, California

Stephen Sheeran
Bishop's University,
Lenoxville, Quebec

Kathy Sherak
San Francisco State
University

Sandra E. Sklarew
Merritt Community College
Oakland, California

Keith Smith
ELS Language Center, San
Francisco

Helen Solorzano
Northeastern University

Jorge Vazquez Solorzano
Bachillerato de la Reina de
Mexico
S. C., Mexico, D. F.,
Mexico

Christina Valdez
Pasadena City College
Pasadena, California

Danielle Valentini
Oakland Community College
Farmington Hills,
Michigan

Amelia Yongue
Howard Community College
Columbia, Maryland

SIMPLE PRESENT
Habits, Routines, and Facts

UNIT GOALS

- Know when to use simple present tense

- Form simple present tense correctly

- Understand the meanings of various adverbs of frequency

- Place adverbs of frequency in correct sentence position

OPENING TASK
How Do You Learn Grammar?

■ STEP 1

How do you prefer to study grammar—in a group with other students, or individually at home?

STEP 2

What do you usually do to learn grammar? Read each statement and say how often you do each of these things. 1 = never 2 = rarely 3 = sometimes 4 = often 5 = always

1. If I don't understand a new grammar point, I . . .
   a. look it up in a grammar book.   1   2   3   4   5
   b. look it up on the Internet.   1   2   3   4   5
   c. ask my teacher.   1   2   3   4   5

2. If I want to practice a new grammar point, I . . .
   a. write some example sentences.   1   2   3   4   5
   b. try to use it in conversation.   1   2   3   4   5
   c. look for examples in a book or a newspaper.   1   2   3   4   5

3. In order to improve my grammar, I . . .
   a. ask my teacher to correct my mistakes.   1   2   3   4   5
   b. ask my friends to correct my mistakes.   1   2   3   4   5
   c. don't worry about mistakes.   1   2   3   4   5

4. I prefer to practice new grammar by . . .
   a. working in a group with classmates.   1   2   3   4   5
   b. listening to and reading grammar explanations.   1   2   3   4   5
   c. making my own examples.   1   2   3   4   5

STEP 3

Compare your answers with another student. Explain the reasons for your answers. Do you like to learn English grammar in the same ways? In what ways are you similar and in what ways are you different? Write a few sentences about how you learn grammar.

Example: *I use the Internet to look up grammar rules, but my partner goes to the library.*

STEP 4

Tell the rest of the class how you and your partner learn English grammar.

Verbs in the Simple Present Tense

use

Habits and Routines

EXAMPLES	EXPLANATIONS
(a) I **ask** questions when I **do not understand**.	*Ask, do not understand*, and *uses* are simple present verbs.
(b) Elzbieta **uses** English as much as possible.	Use the simple present to talk about habits (things you do again and again).
(c) Our classes **start** at 9:00 A.M.	Use the simple present to talk about everyday routines (things you do regularly).
(d) Daniela **goes** to school five days a week.	

EXERCISE 1

Go back to Step 2 of the Opening Task on page 1. Underline all the simple present verbs you can find. Compare your answers with a partner.

form

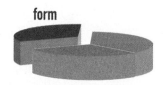

Simple Present Tense

STATEMENT	NEGATIVE	QUESTION	SHORT ANSWER
I / You / We / They } work.	I / You / We / They } do not/don't work.	Do { I / you / we / they } work?	Yes, { I / you / we / they } do.
He / She / It } works.	He / She / It } does not/doesn't work.	Does { he / she / it } work?	Yes, { he / she / it } does.
			No, { I / you / we / they } don't.
			No, { he / she / it } doesn't.

EXERCISE 2

Look at what you wrote in Step 3 of the Opening Task on page 1. Underline all the simple present verbs that you used. Did you use them correctly? Check your answers with a partner and then with your teacher.

EXERCISE 3

STEP 1 What are some *other* things you do and do not do to learn English grammar? Complete the following, using full sentences.

Some things I do:

1. <u>I usually write an example sentence in my notebook.</u>

2. I _____

3. I _____

Some things I don't do:

1. I _____

2. I _____

3. I _____

STEP 2 Get together with a partner, and tell each other about things you do and do not do to learn English grammar. Then, without showing your answers to each other, write about what your partner does and doesn't do.

My partner, (name) _____,
does several different things to learn English grammar. (She/He) _____
_____
_____
_____

STEP 3 Now get together with a different partner. Ask each other what you do to learn English grammar (*Do you* . . . ?). Together with your new partner, decide on the three most useful ways to learn English grammar. Share your ideas with the rest of the class. Write them here:

1. We _____

2. We _____

3. We _____

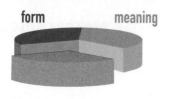

FOCUS 3 | Showing How Often Something Happens

Adverbs of Frequency

EXAMPLES	EXPLANATIONS
(a) Kazue **often** uses a dictionary, but Florian **never** uses one. Most Often (100%) ⬆ always usually often sometimes seldom rarely hardly ever ⬇ never Least Often (0%)	*Often* and *never* are adverbs of frequency. They show how often something happens. For more information on adverbs of frequency, see Unit 18, Focus 5.
(b) **I usually** get up early. (c) He **never** calls me.	Where to put adverbs of frequency: **before** the main verb (b and c)
(d) She is **always** happy. (e) They are **rarely** late.	**after** the verb *be* (d and e)

▪ EXERCISE 4

Which of these things do you do to practice English? Tell your partner. Add some more ideas of your own. Use an adverb of frequency from the chart.

- Use a dictionary?
- Read a grammar book?
- Use the Internet?
- Write in your journal?
- Read the newspaper?

- Play games?
- Write words in a vocabulary notebook?
- ....
- ....
- ....

Example: Student A: *Do you use a dictionary to help you study?*
Student B: *I **rarely** use my dictionary in class, but I **often** look up new words at home.*

EXERCISE 5

STEP 1 Describe a typical day for students in each of these photos. Use the words in the box.

sit in rows	take notes	work in groups
work in pairs	ask questions	raise your hand
answer questions	listen carefully	use computers

1

2

3

4

STEP 2
Read the descriptions below and match each description to a picture on page 5. Write the number of the picture under each description. Compare your answers with a partner.

A We sit in rows, and the teacher stands at the front. The teacher explains grammar rules, and the students listen and take notes. Students sometimes practice their writing in class.

————————

B Our English classes are always very relaxed. We usually work in pairs or small groups and often play games in class to practice our English. These games are a lot of fun and we sometimes laugh a lot. We don't feel nervous about speaking English when we play games.

————————

C We often work on special projects in our English class. We use computers to find information about a topic or we interview people to see what they think. Then we make a presentation about our topic to the rest of the class.

————————

D The students in my English class are very enthusiastic. Every time the teacher asks a question, everybody wants to answer it. We always raise our hands and hope that the teacher will choose us.

————————

STEP 3
How are the classes in the photographs like (or unlike) classes in your country? First, discuss this question with your partner. Then be ready to tell the rest of the class.

EXERCISE 6

STEP 1 Complete the chart about students and teachers in your country and in the United States. The first one about teachers in your country has been done for you as an example. If you do not have enough room to write your answers on the chart, copy the chart into your notebook.

	TEACHERS IN YOUR COUNTRY	STUDENTS IN YOUR COUNTRY	TEACHERS IN THE UNITED STATES	STUDENTS IN THE UNITED STATES /Canada
Usually	stand in front of the class	speak when the teacher lines the class.	standing front of the class.	scream when the bell sound
Sometimes	give us lest homework.	Explain the class by yourselves	send home work.	Arrives a little later, because the weather.
Hardly ever	walk around the class	give the hand to the teacher	speack with the parents, about the child report.	watch some movies in class.
Never	give us time to rest.	stand up when the teacher comes	stand up when the teacher comes.	Play outside in the winter.

STEP 2 Get together with another student from another country, if possible. Ask this partner questions about teachers and students in his or her country.

Example: *Tell me about teachers in your country. Do they usually give a lot of homework? Do they sometimes tell jokes in class?*

STEP 3 Look at the information from your chart and from your partner's chart. Use the information to make as many true sentences as you can.

Example: *Students in my country usually stand up when the teacher comes into the room.*

EXERCISE 7

STEP 1 Get together with a partner. Quickly look at the occupations in the box below.

OCCUPATIONS		
a student	a police officer	a businessperson
an administrative assistant	a flight attendant	a bartender
a mechanic	a teacher	a nurse
an architect	a bus driver	a restaurant server

STEP 2 Read the job descriptions below. Can you match them with the occupations in the box? Write the occupation on the line next to each description.

1. He wears a uniform and usually travels many miles a day. He serves food and drinks, but he hardly ever prepares them himself. _____ *a flight attendant*

2. She works in an office, but she often takes work home with her. She generally earns a high salary, but often feels a lot of stress. She sometimes entertains clients in the evening. _business person_

3. He usually wears a uniform and always carries a gun. He leads a dangerous life, so his job rarely gets boring. _Police Officer_

4. He often works at night and meets many different people. He serves drinks and gets tips when people like his service. _Bartender_

5. She wears a uniform and drives many miles a day. She never serves food and drinks. _Bus Driver_

6. He spends many hours in the classroom and asks questions. He always has a lot of work to do and sometimes writes on the board. _Student_

7. She often wears a uniform and walks many miles a day. She works very hard and does not earn very much money, although she sometimes gets generous tips. _Restaurant Server_

8. He spends a lot of time in the classroom and likes to ask questions. He often writes on the board. _Teacher_

Courhus

STEP 3 Now write similar descriptions for the jobs in the box that are not described above. What do these workers do? _and espend test money._ _(Administrative assistent)_

9. _She always help asist to the businessperron._
10. _He always wear uniform, and fixes cars (mechanic)_
11. _She always wear with blue uniform and asist the Dr._
12. _He desig a house, and earns high salary:_

On your own, think of two more jobs and write a short job description for each one.

13. _____

14. _____

STEP 5   Get together with another student and read your descriptions to each other. Ask and answer questions until you guess the jobs your partner described in Step 4. For example: *Does he or she . . . ? Is he or she a . . . ?*

EXERCISE 8

Sam is looking for a roommate to share his apartment, and Dave is looking for a place to live. They are trying to find out if they will get along as roommates. Complete their conversation, using verbs that fit the meaning of the sentences. Sometimes more than one answer is possible.

Sam: What do you usually do on weekends?

Dave: Well, I usually (1) ____wake up____ early, about 5:30, and then I (2) _____ by the river for an hour or so before breakfast.

Sam: Yeah? And what (3) _____ you _____ next?

Dave: After breakfast, I (4) _____ a cold shower, and then I usually (5) _____ my bike, or I sometimes (6) _____ tennis for a couple of hours. What (7) _____ you _____ on Saturday mornings?

Sam: I like to relax on weekends; I (8) _____ home and (9) _____ the newspaper and (10) _____ TV.

Dave: All weekend?

Sam: No. On Sundays, I often get in my sports car and (11) _____ to the beach.

Dave: Great! I like swimming, too. It's a habit that I learned from my brother. He (12) _____ in the ocean every day of the year, even in the winter.

Sam: Well, I rarely (13) _____ in the ocean. I usually (14) _____ on the beach and try to get a good suntan. Then I (15) _____ some of my friends, and we go to a nightclub and dance.

Dave: Don't you ever exercise?

Sam: Well, I (16) (not) _____ to a health club or gym, but every Saturday night I go to a nightclub, and I (17) _____ for hours. That's my idea of exercise.

Dave: Look, here's the phone number of a friend of mine. He (18) _____ dancing and nightclubs, just like you. Why don't you give him a call and see if he wants to be your roommate?

STEP 1   Talk to your partner about your daily routines. Complete the chart using adverbs of frequency. Would you make good roommates, or not?

Do you wake up early?

	YOU	YOUR PARTNER
Wake up early	I usually wake up early.	Yes, she usually wakes up early.
Sleep late	I usually sleep late.	Yes, she sleeps late usually
Go to bed early	I hardly ever go to bed early.	She sometimes goes to bed early
Stay up late	Sometimes stay up late.	Yes, she usually stays up late.
Go running	I sometimes go running.	Yes she sometimes goes running.
Go to a nightclub	I Hardly ever go to a nightclub	No, she never goes to a nightclub.
Play tennis	I never play tennis.	No, she never plays tennis
Relax at home	I Usually Relax at home.	Yes, she usually relaxs at home.
Watch TV (not "a lot")	I Usually watch my t.u.	Yes, she usually watchs my t.u.
Have friends over	I sometimes have friends Over.	Yes, she hardly ever has friends over.
Read quietly	I Sometimes read quietly.	Yes, she sometimes reads quietly.

STEP 2   Change partners. Tell your new partner about your previous partner.

FOCUS 4   Talking About Facts

use

EXAMPLES	EXPLANATIONS
(a) The sun **rises** in the east and **sets** in the west. (b) Brazilians **speak** Portuguese. (c) Water **boils** at 100° C.	Use the simple present to talk about facts (things that are true).

EXERCISE 10

STEP 1   Match the pictures to the animal names in the box.

Bat.

bear

spider.

elephant

swan

horse.

antelope

scorpion

horse	elephant	spider	bat
bear	swan	scorpion	antelope

What do you know about these animals? Be ready to tell the rest of the class anything that you know.

STEP 2
Get together with a partner and draw lines connecting the animals in Column A with appropriate information about them in Column B. Don't worry if you are not sure of all the answers. With your partner, decide what you think is probably the best match for each piece of information.

A	B
1. Horses	live for about two years. 3
2. Bats	sometimes go for four days without water. 4
3. Scorpions	stay with the same mates all their lives. 5
4. Elephants	use their ears to "see." 2
5. Swans	have twelve eyes. 8
6. Antelopes	sleep during the winter months. 7
7. Bears	sleep standing up. 1
8. Spiders	run at 70 miles per hour. 6

STEP 3
Get together with another pair and compare your answers. When you are ready, compare your answers with the rest of the class. As a class, decide on what you think are probably the best answers. Then check your answers on page A-14.

STEP 4
Do you know any other unusual facts about these animals or any other animals? Tell the rest of the class about them.

Use Your English

ACTIVITY 1 speaking/listening

The purpose of this activity is to prove or disprove the following statements about your classmates. Stand up, walk around the room, and ask your classmates questions to see if the following are true (T) or false (F).

1. Most of the people in this room do not eat breakfast.   T   (F)
2. Women drink more coffee than men.   (T)   F
3. Fifty percent of the people in this room watch TV at night.   (T)   F
4. Somebody in this room wears contact lenses.   T   F
5. More than three people read a newspaper in English every day.   (T)   F
6. More than 50 percent of the people in this room drive a car.   (T)   F
7. Nobody likes opera.   T   (F)
8. More than two people here come to school by bike.   T   (F)
9. Everybody gets more than six hours of sleep a night.   T   F
10. Most of the people in this room have a sister.   T   F

ACTIVITY 2 speaking/listening/writing

Interview someone about his or her job. Find out three things he or she sometimes does, often does, and never does. Write a description of the job based on your interview. What is your opinion of the job? Is it different from or similar to what you expected?

ACTIVITY 3 speaking/listening

The purpose of this activity is to find out what people usually do on certain special days.

■ **STEP 1**   Form a team with one or two other students, and choose one of the special days from the chart below.

■ **STEP 2**   Tell the rest of the class which special day your team has chosen. Make sure that there is at least one team for each special day.

■ **STEP 3**   With your team, interview three different people (native speakers of English if possible). Find out what they do or what they think usually happens on this special day. Make notes on the chart below or in your notebook. If possible, record your interviews.

■ **STEP 4**   After doing your interviews, use your notes to tell the rest of the class what your team found.

New Year's Eve _____

Valentine's Day

Halloween _____

Thanksgiving Day

■ **STEP 5**   Listen to your recorded interview, or use your notes to identify and write down any sentences that contain the simple present tense or adverbs of frequency.

ACTIVITY 4 listening

CD Tracks 1,2,3

STEP 1

Listen to the audio of people describing what they do on certain special days. Which special days do you think each speaker is talking about? Write your answers under "Special Day" in the chart below.

SPEAKER	SPECIAL DAY	VERBS IN THE SIMPLE PRESENT TENSE
Speaker 1		
Speaker 2		
Speaker 3		

STEP 2

Listen to the audio again. On the right side of the chart, write down as many examples of verbs in the simple present tense as you can.

ACTIVITY 5 speaking/listening

Prepare a short talk for your classmates, describing a special day or holiday that people celebrate in your country, city, or region. Talk about what people usually do on this day and how they celebrate. Don't forget to include an introduction to your talk. For example: *I am going to tell you about a very special holiday in my country. The name of the holiday is. . . .* If possible, record your talk and listen after class.

■ **STEP 1** Complete the following with information that is true about yourself. Write complete sentences.

Something I usually do in summer	
Something I often do on weekends	
Something I rarely do in this country	
Something I sometimes do on Fridays	

■ **STEP 2** Memorize these four sentences about yourself.

■ **STEP 3** Walk around the room. When your teacher tells you to stop, find the nearest person. Tell the person your four sentences and listen to that person's sentences. Then memorize each other's sentences.

■ **STEP 4** Walk around the room. When your teacher tells you to stop, find a different person. Tell this new person about the last person you spoke to. Then listen to that person's sentences. Do not talk about yourself. Memorize what he or she tells you.

■ **STEP 5** Find someone different. Tell him or her the information the last person told you. Listen to the new person's sentences. Memorize what he or she tells you.

■ **STEP 6** Now find someone new. Continue the process for as long as possible. Remember, you always pass along the information the last person tells you. Try to speak to as many different people as possible.

■ **STEP 7** At the end, tell the rest of the class the information you heard from the last person. Is all the information true?

ACTIVITY 7 writing

Write a description of a typical high school classroom in your country. For example, what does the room look like? Where do the students sit? Where does the teacher sit? Is there any special equipment in the room? What is on the walls? What do teachers and students usually do when they are in the classroom?

ACTIVITY 8 research on the web

 On the Web: Use an Internet search engine such as Google® or Yahoo® to find out about a celebration or holiday in another country. When does it take place? What do people usually wear/eat/do? If you want, you can research one of these examples: Mardi Gras (Brazil), Obon (Japan), Inti Raymi (Peru), Songkran (Thailand).

ACTIVITY 9 reflection

Think of one study skill that you would like to improve. Describe in detail how you usually practice this study skill. Try to break your description down into several different steps. Read your description to your partner.

Example: <u>Writing an essay:</u> First, I get out my notebooks, dictionary, and grammar book. Then I find some sheets of rough paper. I sharpen all my pencils. Then I . . .

PRESENT PROGRESSIVE AND SIMPLE PRESENT

Actions and States

UNIT GOALS

- Know when to use present progressive

- Form present progressive correctly

- Choose between simple present and present progressive

- Know which verbs are not usually used in the present progressive

OPENING TASK

What's Happening?

◼ STEP 1

A typical day at the office includes short conversations. Look at the picture. Where is this conversation happening? What are they discussing?

◼ STEP 2

Work with a partner. Student A will look at picture A on the next page. Student B will look at picture B on page A-14. There are ten differences between the pictures. What are they?

Example:

Student A: *The woman at the front is opening a letter.*

Student B: *No, she isn't. She's writing a letter.*

Picture A

FOCUS 1 | Present Progressive: Actions in Progress

use

EXAMPLES	EXPLANATIONS
(a) Right now, **I am sitting** on the couch and my brothers **are cooking** dinner. (b) It **is raining** and Oscar **is waiting** for the bus.	*Am sitting* and *are cooking* are present progressive forms. Use the present progressive to describe an action that is in progress and happening at the time of speaking.
(c) This semester, **I am taking** three math classes. (d) Their baby **is waking up** very early these days.	Use the present progressive for an action that is happening **around** the time of speaking, but not happening **exactly** at that time.
At time of speaking: *right now* *at the moment* *today* *at present*	Around time of speaking: *this year* *this semester* *this week* *these days*	These time expressions are often used with the present progressive.

■ EXERCISE 1

STEP 1   Read the following statements about picture A in the Opening Task. Without looking back at the picture, which statements are true (T) and which ones are false (F)?

1. Two women are talking on the phone.   T   F
2. Three men are wearing jackets.   T   F
3. Two people standing.   T   F
4. Two men are reading.   T   F
5. Three people are talking.   T   F
6. One man is drinking coffee.   T   F

STEP 2   Now look at picture A and check your answers. How many of your answers were correct?

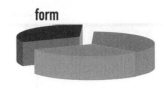
form

Present Progressive

To form the present progressive, use *be* + present participle (*-ing*) of the main verb:

STATEMENT	NEGATIVE	QUESTION	SHORT ANSWER
I am (I'm) working.	I am not (I'm not) working.	Am I working?	Yes, I am. No, I'm not.
You are (you're) working.	You are not (aren't) working.	Are you working?	Yes, you are. No, you aren't. (No, you're not.)
She/He/It is (She's/He's/It's) working.	She/He/It is not (isn't) working.	Is she/he/it working?	Yes, she/he/it is. No, she/he/it isn't. (No, she's/he's/it's not.)
We are (We're) working.	We are not (aren't) working.	Are we working?	Yes, we are. No, we aren't. (No, we're not.)
They are (They're) working	They are not (aren't) working.	Are they working?	Yes, they are. No, they aren't. (No, they're not.)

 EXERCISE 2

Study the picture on page 19 for one minute. Close your book and, from memory, write as many sentences as possible to describe what is happening in the picture. Compare your sentences with those of the rest of the class. Who can remember the most?

FOCUS 3 — Simple Present or Present Progressive?

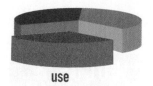

use

EXAMPLES	EXPLANATIONS	
	Simple Present	**Present Progressive**
(a) Philippe **watches** six TV programs a day.	For an action that happens regularly, again and again. (See Unit 1.)	
(b) A: Where's Philippe? B: In his room. He's **watching** TV. (c) Leanne can't come to the phone right now because she's **taking** a shower.		For an action that is in progress **at** the time of speaking.
(d) Philippe **is watching** more TV than usual these days (e) Audrey **is learning** Greek this semester.		For an action in progress **around** the time of speaking.
(f) Carmina **lives** in Mexico City. (g) The sun **rises** in the east. (h) Mark always **reads** the sports section of the newspaper first.	For facts, situations, and states that we do not expect to change.	
(i) Angela **is living** with her mother for the time being. (Someday she will move into a house of her own.) (j) Matt will start college next year. Until then, he **is working** at Fat Burger.		For situations and actions that are temporary and that we expect to change.
(k) Cell phones **are becoming** more popular these days.		For situations and actions that are changing.

EXERCISE 3

Check (✓) the sentence (*a* or *b*) that is closest in meaning to the first statement. Compare your answers with a partner.

1. I live in New York now.
   a. New York is my home.
   b. I expect to move very soon.

2. I'm staying with a friend.
   a. I'm at my friend's house right now.
   b. I won't stay at my friend's house for long.

3. I start work early in the morning.
   a. I usually start work early every day.
   b. I start work earlier than usual these days.

4. I'm walking to work these days.
   a. I'm walking to work right now.
   b. I started walking to work recently.

5. I'm writing to you on my computer at work.
   a. I am writing at this moment.
   b. I usually write letters on my computer.

6. Oh, no! The boss is coming over to my desk.
   a. The boss is walking towards my desk right now.
   b. The boss visits my desk quite often.

7. Many students are using wireless Internet in cafés.
   a. Many students are using computers in cafés these days.
   b. Many students are using computers in cafés right now.

8. The receptionist makes the coffee at work.
   a. He makes the coffee every day.
   b. He is making the coffee night now.

Complete the following sentences using either the simple present or the present progressive. Use a form of the verb in parentheses. The first one has been done for you.

Melissa: Hello?

Chris: Oh hi! Is Angie there?

Melissa: Hi, Chris. It's Melissa. Angie's here, but she (1) _____is taking_____ (take) a shower at the moment. How are you? What (2) _____ you _____ (do) these days?

Chris: I (3) _____ (study) business management this semester. How about you?

Melissa: I (4) _____ (take) computers and Spanish. I _____ (work) part-time at the computer store for a few weeks.

Chris: I (5) _____ (speak) Spanish, but I'm terrible at computers. In fact, I _____ (have) trouble with my computer right now.

Melissa: I could help you, if you like.

Chris: Sure! (6) _____ you _____ (have) time today? What time (7) _____ you _____ (finish) work?

Melissa: At around 3 P.M. on Saturdays, but I usually (8) _____ (not, get) home till around 4.

Chris: OK, let's meet at 4:30.

When people send text messages by phone, they often use just the first letters of each word to make the messages shorter. Can you translate the following into written English? Write your answers below.

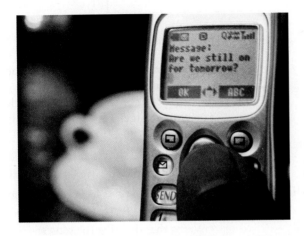

Key:
B = believe, C = see,
D = don't, H = hear,
I = I, it
K = know, L = later, love
M = mean, N = next,
O = or, N = not,
R = are, S = so,
T = think, U = you,
W = what, welcome

1. **CUL** _See you later_
2. **IHU**
3. **KWIM?**
4. **ILU**
5. **IDTS**
6. **IDK**
7. **BION**
8. **URW**

You can find the answers on page A-15.

Now underline all the verbs from your answers. Write them in the appropriate boxes below. The first one has been done for you.

VERBS THAT EXPRESS EMOTIONS AND FEELINGS	VERBS THAT EXPRESS SENSES AND PERCEPTIONS	VERBS THAT EXPRESS COGNITION: KNOWLEDGE THOUGHTS, AND BELIEFS
	See	

Which verb does not fit these categories? _____

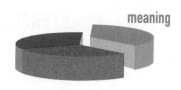

FOCUS 4	Verbs Not Usually Used in the Progressive

EXAMPLES	EXPLANATIONS
(a) He **loves** me, but he **hates** my cat. (b) NOT: He is loving me, but he is hating my cat. (c) I **know** your sister. (d) NOT: I am knowing your sister.	Some verbs are not usually used in the progressive. The reason is that they describe states or situations that we do not expect to change. They do not describe actions.
(e) Hugo **likes** opera, but his girlfriend **prefers** ballet. (f) Those flowers **smell** wonderful! (g) I **think** the President has some interesting ideas about health care, but many people **believe** he is wrong. (h) Please be careful with that vase. It **belongs** to my aunt. (i) A: Are you going to buy that radio? B: No, it **costs** too much.	Common nonprogressive (stative) verbs: • Verbs that express feelings and emotions: *love prefer hate like appreciate want dislike* • Verbs that describe the senses: *see hear taste smell* • Verbs that express knowledge, opinions, and beliefs: *think believe know understand* • Verbs that express possession: *have belong own possess* • Other common nonprogressive verbs: *be seem owe exist need appear cost weigh*

EXERCISE 6

Complete the following with the simple present or the present progressive, using the verbs in parentheses.

Technology (1) __is changing__ (change) the way we communicate. Today, more and more people (2) _____ (own) cell phones. Look around you. How many people (3) _____ (use) a cell phone right now? Cell phones (4) _____ (give) us a feeling of safety. We never (5) _____ (feel) lonely. Cell phones (6) _____ (become) popular with teenagers, too. They often (7) _____ (send) hundreds of text messages every day. They (8) _____ (think) they will be unpopular if they (9) _____ (not, have) a cell phone. People (10) _____ (talk) to each other more these days, but (11) _____ they _____ (understand) each other better?

use

EXAMPLES	EXPLANATIONS
(a) I **love** you. (b) I **hate** my job. (c) She **knows** a lot about the history of her country.	Nonprogressive verbs usually describe a state or quality that we do not expect to change. They do not describe actions.
State / **Action** (d) I **weigh** 120 pounds. / I **am weighing** myself (to see if I've gained weight). (e) Mmm! Dinner **smells** great! / I'm **smelling** the milk (to see if it smells fresh). (f) This soup **tastes** good. / He **is tasting** the soup (to see if it needs salt).	Some verbs describe both a state **and** an action. If the verb describes a state, use the simple present. If the verb describes an action, use the present progressive.
(g) David **is** very polite. (h) Tanya **is** a little shy.	Do not use *be* in the progressive when it describes a state or quality you do not expect to change.
(i) We **have** two cars. (j) NOT: We are having two cars. (k) We **are having fun.** (l) We always **have fun** on vacation.	Do not use *have* in the progressive to describe possession. However, you can use *have* in the progressive to describe an experience. Use the progressive if the experience is in progress at or around the time of speaking (k). Use the simple present if the experience happens again and again (l). Common expressions using *have* to describe an experience: *have fun* *have a good time* *have problems* *have trouble with* *have difficulty with*
(m) I can't talk to you right now because I **have** a really sore throat. (n) NOT: I am having a sore throat. (o) Sandy **has** a headache and a high fever today. Maybe she **has** the flu. (p) NOT: Sandy is having a headache and a high fever today. Maybe she is having the flu.	Do not use *have* in the progressive to describe a medical problem or physical discomfort.

Work with a partner or in a small group. You need a die and a small object (like a coin) to represent each person. Each person will also need a piece of paper and a pen or pencil.

STEP 1 Take turns throwing the die. The person who throws the highest number starts.

STEP 2 Put your coins (or objects) on the square marked "Start" on the following page.

STEP 3 Throw the die and move your coin that number of squares.

STEP 4 Complete the sentence in the square you land on by saying the answer out loud. If everyone agrees with your answer, you may write it on a piece of paper with your name and take another turn. If the class is not sure, the teacher will be the referee. If you make a mistake or do not know the answer, the next person gets a turn. The winner is the first person to reach the final square.

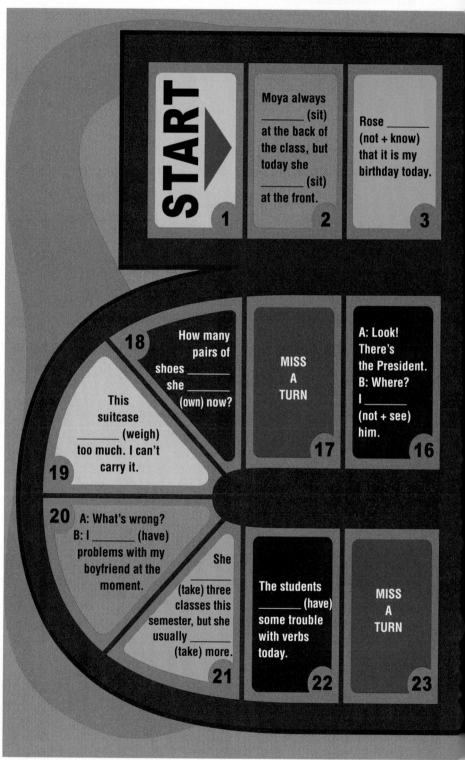

START

1

Moya always _____ (sit) at the back of the class, but today she _____ (sit) at the front.
2

Rose _____ (not + know) that it is my birthday today.
3

18 How many pairs of shoes _____ she _____ (own) now?

MISS A TURN
17

A: Look! There's the President. B: Where? I _____ (not + see) him.
16

19 This suitcase _____ (weigh) too much. I can't carry it.

20 A: What's wrong? B: I _____ (have) problems with my boyfriend at the moment.

She _____ (take) three classes this semester, but she usually _____ (take) more.
21

The students _____ (have) some trouble with verbs today.
22

MISS A TURN
23

4 MISS A TURN

5 People _____ (spend) less money on entertainment these days.

6 What _____ you _____ (think) Henry _____ (think) about right now?

7 Mmm! Is that a new perfume? You _____ (smell) great.

8 MISS A TURN

9 A: How are the kids? B: They both _____ (have) sore throats today.

10 A: Shhh! We _____ (study) for a test.

11 A: _____ you _____ (like) Mexican food? B: Yes, I _____ (love) It!

12 A: How's Joe? B: Great. He _____ (have) fun because he _____ (have) a new car.

13 A: Where's Tim? B: I _____ (think) he _____ (take) a nap.

14 A: _____ you always _____ (take) the bus? B: No, I usually _____ (walk) to work.

15 A: _____ you _____ (like) your job? B. No, I _____ (hate) it.

24 She _____ (write) a letter now, but she rarely _____ (write) letters.

25 I _____ (love) grammar!

26 A: The chef _____ (taste) the food right now. B: Is it good? A: Yes! It _____ (taste) wonderful!

27 MISS A TURN

28 Did you cut your hand? It _____ (bleed).

29 END

Use Your English

ACTIVITY 1 listening/writing

In this activity, you will hear a teacher describe a Resource Center.

CD Track 4

■ **STEP 1**   Before you listen, write down three things that you expect students to be doing in the Resource Center.

■ **STEP 2**   Listen to the audio again. Write down examples of simple present and present progressive verbs in the chart below.

SIMPLE PRESENT	PRESENT PROGRESSIVE

ACTIVITY 2 writing/listening

Go to a crowded place where you can sit, watch, and listen to what is happening around you. Look carefully at everything that is happening. Pretend you are a journalist or a radio or television reporter. Describe in writing everything that you see. Do not forget to include everything you hear as well.

ACTIVITY 3 speaking/listening

Do you know how to play tic-tac-toe? In this activity, you will be playing a version of this well-known game. Work with a partner or in teams.

■ **STEP 1** Copy each of the following onto separate cards or different pieces of paper.

she/speak	she/dance (?)*	you/live
we/hear	we/sing	I/see
I/understand	they/work (?)*	
they/eat	he/believe	
they/think about	you/write (?)*	(?)* = make a question

■ **STEP 2** Place the cards face down on the table in front of you.

■ **STEP 3** Player or Team X chooses a square from the box below and picks up a card from the pile. The player must make a meaningful statement that includes the word(s) in the square and the word(s) on the card. If the card has a "?" on it, the player must ask a question. Each statement or question must contain at least four words, not including the words in the square. Use the simple present or present progressive.

every day	today	usually
this week	occasionally	right now
often	at the moment	sometimes

■ **STEP 4** If everyone accepts the statement, Player or Team X marks the square with an X.

■ **STEP 5** Player or Team O then chooses a different square and takes a new card. The Player or Team O makes a statement. If the statement is correct, Player or Team O marks the square with an O.

■ **STEP 6** The first person or team to have three Xs or three Os in a straight line wins. You can play this game again and again by erasing the Xs and Os at the end of each round, or by writing them on small pieces of paper and covering the squares with these. Good luck!

ACTIVITY 4 speaking/listening/writing

STEP 1

Go around the classroom and try to find a different person for each of the situations in the chart below. Write the person's name in the box marked *Name* and add more information in the box marked *Information.* We have given some suggestions here, but you probably have more ideas of your own.

SITUATION	NAME	INFORMATION
. . . is reading a book in English		*Title? His/her opinion?*
. . . regularly reads a newspaper from his/her country		*Why?*
. . . reads more than one book a month (in any language)		*Favorite books?*
. . . usually goes to the movies several times a month		*How often? Favorite movie?*
. . . is wearing an article of clothing made in the U.S.A.		*Describe it.*
. . . regularly plays a musical instrument		*What kind? How often?*
. . . is wearing perfume or cologne at the moment		*What kind? Describe it.*
. . . has a pet		*What kind? How old?*

■ **STEP 2**   Look at all the information that you collected. Choose three or four of the most interesting or surprising things that you learned about your classmates and write about this information. Remember to include an introduction. For example: *I interviewed some of my classmates and I learned several new things about them. First, I learned that Maria likes to read. In fact, she is reading a book in English that she is enjoying very much. . . .*

Read your report to a partner. Ask your partner to listen first to count the examples of the **simple present** and then listen again, doing the same for the **present progressive.**

ACTIVITY 5 writing

Journal Entry: What things are changing in your country? What things are getting more popular? What things are disappearing? How do you feel about it?

ACTIVITY 6 research on the web

On the Web: Use an Internet search engine such as Google® or Yahoo® to find out about events that are happening right now in your town or neighborhood. Type the name of your city or town and "current events." Choose one event that you like and tell your class or a partner about it.

ACTIVITY 7 reflection

How do you use technology in your studies? How are your study habits changing because of technology? Write a journal entry about how you feel about these changes.

TALKING ABOUT THE FUTURE

Be Going To and *Will*

- Form statements and questions about the future using *be going to* and *will*

- Know the uses of *be going* to and *will*

- Choose between *be going to* and *will*

OPENING TASK
Telling Your Future

Some people believe that you can see your future in the lines of your palm. Palm reading is the art of telling your future by looking at your palm. What is your opinion of palm reading?

■ STEP 1

Read the meanings connected with each line on page 35.

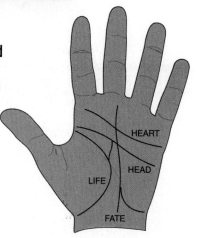

nanys 4 hirgo.com.
Fate = Destino.

Life Line:

Does a line cross your life line? You will have a big change in your life. You are going to move, change schools or jobs, or marry.

Does your life line split into two branches? Your life will be full of adventure.

Does it bend towards your little finger? You are going to have a pleasant and quiet life.

Head Line:

Does it go straight across? You will be a lawyer, a doctor, or a scientist.

Does it curve down? You will be an artist, a musician, or a dancer.

Heart Line:

Is it close to your head line? You will have a few close friends.

Is there a wide space between your heart and head lines? You will be friends with many different people.

Fate Line:

going down. *I did what I want to do.*

Is it a straight downward line? You will achieve all your goals.

Does it bend towards your first finger? You are going to be successful.

something very good happen

■ STEP 2

Use the information to make predictions about each person's future.

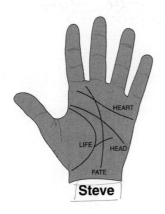

Steve

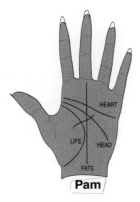

Pam

■ STEP 3

Look at your partner's palm. Make predictions about your partner's future.

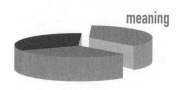

FOCUS 1 | Talking About the Future with *Will* and *Be Going To*

EXAMPLES	EXPLANATIONS
(a) Your life **is going to** be full of adventure. OR	Use either *be going to* or *will* to make a prediction or talk about the future.
(b) Your life **will** be full of adventure.	
(c) You **are going to** be sucessful. OR	
(d) You **will** be sucessful.	

EXERCISE 1

Write predictions about yourself and your partner using the information from the Opening Task.

Example: *My partner's life will be full of adventure.*

Martime 1. _She will archieve all think that she wants._

Fernanda 2. _She will be an famous artist._

Jorge 3. _He's life will be full of adventure and he is going to meets important people._

Taman 4.

5. _She will be friends with many people around the world._

6. _____

Check your sentences. Did you use *will* and *be going to* correctly?

Will = No Cambia" form

FOCUS 2 *Will* and *Be Going To*

going = Change:

Will does not change to agree with the subject:

STATEMENT		NEGATIVE			QUESTION		
I You We They She He It	will leave. 'll	I You We They She He It	will not won't	leave.	Will	I you we they she he it	leave?

Be going to changes to agree with the subject:

STATEMENT		NEGATIVE		QUESTION		
I	am going to leave. 'm	I	am not 'm not going to leave.	Am (em)	I (ay)	going to leave?
You We They	are going to leave. 're	You We They	are not aren't going to leave. 're not	Are	you we they	going to leave?
She He It	is going to leave. 's	He She It	is not isn't going to leave. 's not	Is	he she it	going to leave?

EXERCISE 2

Pill

Disease
- Elnes.

STEP 1 **Imagine our world 100 years from now. Write yes/no questions about what life will be like.**

Example: Will we live in houses with solar energy for electricity?

1. will we have foods pills?
2. will we have robots as housekeping?
3. will have life in marte?
4. will be posible drive a flying car?

STEP 2 Ask your partner the questions from Step 1 and write down his or her answers. Think of what things we are going to have and also things we are *not* going to have.

Example: No. We aren't going to live in houses with solar electricity. We will live in houses under the sea.

1. Yes, we will have. food pill.
2. Yes we will have. robots housekeaping?
3. Yes, we will, life.
4. Yes, we will

FOCUS 3   Making Predictions: *Will* or *Be Going To?*

use

EXAMPLES	EXPLANATIONS
(a) Be careful! That chair **is going** to break.	It is better to use *be going to* for actions or events that you think will happen very soon or immediately
(b) NOT: Be careful! That chair will break!	
(c) Oh no!! That little boy **is going to** fall off the bridge	
(d) NOT: Oh no!! That little boy will fall off the bridge.	
(e) *Babysitter to child:* Your mommy's **going to** be very angry about this.	When the future event or action will not happen immediately: It is better to use *be going to* in informal situations (relaxed and friendly situations, with family or friends). In informal speech, *going to* is usually pronounced *gonna*.
(f) *Student to professor:* **Will** the test be difficult? *Professor:* It **will** be tough, but I don't think you **will** have too many problems with it.	It is better to use *will* in more formal situations.

38   UNIT 3

EXERCISE 3

For each of the following, decide on the best form to use: *be going to* or *will*. In some sentences, it is possible to use both. The first one has been done for you.

1. Quick! Catch the baby! I think he ___is going to___ roll off the bed.

2. Excuse me, Mr. President. Do you think unemployment ___is going to___ decrease in the foreseeable future? *soon.*

3. Oh, no! Look at those clouds. It ___is going to___ rain. ✓

4. I predict that you ___will be___ meet a tall, dark, and handsome stranger, and you ___will___ fall in love and get married.

5. One day we ___will___ look back at all this and laugh.

6 I don't believe it. Look at Paula! I think she ___is going to___ ask that guy to dance with her.

7. A: What do you think about my son's chances of getting into Harvard, Dr. Heath?

   B: I don't think he ___will___ have any problems at all, Mrs. Lee.

8. Meteorologists predict that the drought ___is going to___ end sometime this fall. ✓
   weather

FOCUS 4 — Future Plans and Intentions: *Be Going To*

use

EXAMPLES	EXPLANATIONS
(a) What **are** you **going to** do this summer? (b) We're **going to** spend the month of August in Italy. We bought the tickets last week, and we're **going to** leave on August 2nd.	It is better to use *be going to* to talk about a future plan or an intention (something you want to do in the future). This shows that you made the decision to do this **before** speaking.

EXERCISE 4

In this exercise, you need to get information from one of your classmates. Use *be going to* or *will* in your answers, as appropriate.

1. Get together with a partner and find out three things he or she intends to do after class:
   My partner ___is going to her home; eat dinner, watch tv___

2. Now find out three things he or she does not intend to do after class:
   My partner ___isn't going to the beach, to Downtown, to shopping.___

3. Now find out three possible plans that he or she has for this weekend:
My partner _isn't going to bbg, Houe ...y Night Club,_

Finally, look back at what you have written in this exercise. Where did you choose *be going to* and where did you choose *will*? Why did you make these choices?

EXERCISE 5

Read the following conversation between two friends carefully and decide if the use of *be going to* or *will* is more appropriate. Check (✓) the sentences you think are acceptable. Correct the sentences you think are unacceptable.

A: (1) _✓_ What are you going to do next year? (2) _✗_ Are you going to go to college?

B: (3) _✗_ Yes! I'm going to go to college in California. I sent in my application six months ago. (4) _✓_ I'll study nursing.

A: (5) _✓_ Fantastic! You'll be a very good nurse.

B: Thanks. What are your plans?

A: I'm not sure. (6) _✓_ I'm going to wait until I get my exam results. (7) _✗_ I'll work during my vacation. I already have a part-time job at the sports center.

B: That sounds good. Did you hear the news about Stan? (8) _✓_ He's going to get married!

A: That's wonderful news! (9) _✗_ Is he going to invite us?

use

FOCUS 5

Two More Uses of *Will*: Making Quick Decisions and Serious Promises

EXAMPLES	EXPLANATIONS
(a) A: I think there's someone at the front door. B: I'll go and check (b) A: Telephone! B: OK. I'll get it. (c) A: I need someone to help out at the recycling center. B: Oh, I **will**!	Use *will* for quick decisions or for something you have decided to do at that moment. The contracted '*ll* is usually used in these situations. Do not use '*ll* in short answers.
(d) I **will** always love you. (e) I'll give you my homework tomorrow, I promise! (f) A: Remember, this is top secret. B: I **won't** tell anybody. You can count on me.	Use *will* to make a serious promise. *Will* + *not* = *won't*

EXERCISE 6

Complete the following, using a form of *be going to* or *will,* as appropriate. The first is an example.

A: What (1) __are you going to__ (you) do tonight?

B: The World Cup Final (2) _____ be on TV at 6:30. Julie

(3) _____ come over and watch it with me.

A: Oh really? Who do you think (4) __is going to__ win?

B: The newspapers say Brazil (5) __is going to__ win. But I think Mexico

(6) _____ give them a good match. What (7) __are you going__
(you) do tonight?

A: I (8) __'m going to.__ go to the movies with Fran. I (9) __am going to__ be
home around 11.

B: You'd better take your umbrella. It looks like it (10) __is going to.__ rain any
minute.

A: Thanks. Can I take yours? I promise I (11) _____ lose it!

B: Sure. I (12) _____ go look for it in the closet.

EXERCISE 7

With a partner, look at these situations and decide on ways to respond using *will* or *be going to*.

1. You look out of the window and notice there are a lot of stormy, black clouds in the sky. What do you say?

   Example: We are going to need an umbrella.

   _____

2. Your friend Oscar is interested in music and in physics, but he can't decide which one to major in next year. After a lot of thought and discussion, he has finally decided to major in music. What does he say to his family?

   1. I am going to be a musician.
   2. I am going to study music.

3. Your friend is organizing an international potluck. She needs people to bring food from different countries. You want to help. What will you promise to do? What are you going to bring or cook?

   I will bring food with you.
   I am going to cook.

4. It's 6:30 A.M. You have to drive to the airport to pick up your uncle at 7:30 A.M., but your car won't start. Your roommate offers to lend you hers, but she needs to have it back by 9:00 A.M. to get to work. What do you tell her?

   thank, I'm going to give it back at this time.

5. You are standing in line in the campus cafeteria. You notice that the backpack of the student in front of you is open and all her books are about to fall out. What do you tell her?

   Excuse me, your books are going to fall out because your backpack is open.

6. One of your classmates is sick and has to go to the doctor's office. He is very worried about missing his history class. You are also in that class. What can you say to reassure him?

   Take care, I'm going to lend you my book and you can have it. the lesson.

7. Your friend is giving you a ride home. Suddenly you notice a little boy who is about to run into the road. Your friend hasn't seen him. What do you say?

Slow Down, You are going to Hit the boy.

8. Your friend Frank loves ballet. He has just bought the last ticket for a special gala performance of *Swan Lake* next Saturday night. You ask him about his plans for the weekend. What does he say?

I'm going to a special gala of ballet.

9. You have promised to do the dishes and clean up the kitchen after dinner. Just before you get started, you receive an unexpected phone call from a friend whose car has broken down, and he urgently needs your help. As you are leaving, your roommate comes into the room and asks, "What about the dishes?" What do you say?

Soory, I promese! I'm going to do the Dishes when I came bak.

10. Madame Cassandra is a fortune-teller who makes exciting predictions about the future. Your teacher is consulting Madame Cassandra. What does Madame Cassandra tell your teacher?

OH! You will have a world of adventure, your live is going to be sucesfull and exciting.

Use Your English

The purpose of this activity is to collect as much information as possible about the future plans and intentions of your classmates. Look at the chart below. Complete as many squares as you can by finding the required information. *Maybe* and *I don't know* are not acceptable answers! Write the information in the appropriate square as well as the name or names of the people who gave you the information. The first person to get information for three squares in a row in any direction is the winner. Good luck!

Find someone who is going to take the TOEFL® test* soon. When is she or he going to take it?	Find three people who are going to cook dinner tonight. What are they going to cook?	Find two people who are going to go to the library after this class. What are they going to do there?
Find two people who are going to play the same sport this week. What sport are they going to play?	Find someone who is going to move to another city within a year. What city is she or he going to move to?	Find someone who is going to go to the movies today. What movie is she or he going to see?
Find someone who is going to get his or her hair cut in the next two weeks. Where is she or he going to get it cut?	Find two people who are going to watch TV tonight. What are they going to watch?	Find two people who are going to celebrate their birthdays next month. What are their birth dates?

*TOEFL is a registered trademark of the Educational Testing Service (ETS). This publication is not endorsed or approved by ETS.

ACTIVITY 2 writing/speaking

■ **STEP 1** Write predictions about the future for your teacher and five of your classmates. Write each prediction on a small slip of paper, and give each one to the appropriate person.

■ **STEP 2** The people who receive predictions will read them aloud, and the rest of the class will decide if they think the predictions will come true.

ACTIVITY 3 writing

What are your predictions for the next ten years? What do you think will happen in the world? What do you think will happen in your country?

■ **STEP 1** Write a brief report on your predictions. Your report should include a short introduction to your topic. It is not necessary to use *will* and *be going to* in every sentence you write!

■ **STEP 2** When you finish writing, read your report carefully and check your use of *will* and *be going to*. Remember, it is often possible to use either one.

  We have written the beginning of a report to give you some ideas, but you probably have better ideas of your own.

LIFE IN THE FUTURE

Nobody knows exactly what will happen in the future, but in my opinion, there will be many important changes in the world in the next ten years. Some of them will be good and some of them will be bad. In this short report, I am going to talk about some of my predictions for the future of the world, as well as the future of my country.

  First, let me tell you about my predictions for the world ...

ACTIVITY 4 speaking/listening

CD Track 5

■ **STEP 1** Listen to the audio of an interviewer and three students talking about their goals and future plans. About how old do you think each speaker is? Take a guess. Take notes on what each speaker says in the chart below

SPEAKER	AGE	FUTURE PLANS AND GOALS
Student 1		
Student 2		
Student 3		

■ **STEP 2** Think about your own goals and future plans. Are they similar to those of any of the three speakers? Explain to a partner.

■ **STEP 3** Listen to the audio again. Write down all the examples you hear of the future with *will* and *be going to*.

ACTIVITY 5 speaking/listening

■ **STEP 1** In this activity, you will interview several people about their goals and future plans. Interview at least three young people who are at different stages of their lives: college students, high school students, and children. Find out what they are going to do when they leave school. Take notes about their goals and plans or, if possible, record your interviews.

■ **STEP 2** Make a list of the most interesting plans and share them with the rest of the class. Report your findings to the class.

■ **STEP 3** (Optional) If you recorded the interviews, listen to the recording and take note of the different ways these native speakers talk about the future. What verb forms do they use to express the future?

ACTIVITY 6 listening/speaking

In this activity, you will create a chain story about your teacher's next vacation.

■ **STEP 1**   Your teacher will start by telling you where he or she is going to go for his or her next vacation and one thing he or she is going to do:

Teacher: *I'm going to go to Hawaii for my vacation, and I am going to climb a mountain.*

■ **STEP 2**   The next person repeats the first part and adds another statement about the teacher's vacation until everyone in the room has added to the description.

Student 1: Ms. O'Neill is going to Hawaii. She is going to climb a mountain. She is going to swim in the ocean, too.

ACTIVITY 7 research on the web

On the Web: Choose one type of technology that you are interested in: for example, cameras, cars, computers, music players, or video games. Use an Internet search engine such as Google® or Yahoo® to research new developments. How will this type of technology be different in the future? How will it affect our lives?

ACTIVITY 8 reflection

Think of three ways you would like to improve your study skills. Write an action plan. What skills are you going to improve? How are you going to work on them?

ASKING QUESTIONS
Yes/No, Wh-, Tag, and Choice Questions

UNIT GOALS

- Understand formation of different types of questions

- Understand meaning of different types of questions

- Recognize the uses of different intonation patterns for various question types

OPENING TASK
Any Questions?

■ STEP 1

What kinds of questions do you ask in class? Work with a partner to make a list of useful questions for learning English.

■ STEP 2

What questions could you ask the teacher in the newspaper article? Work alone or with other students to complete the questions on the facing page.

South City College 2006 Teacher of the Year!

Teacher of the Year

Congratulations to Elena Dominguez, who was named Teacher of the Year. Elena was born in Venezuela and now lives in South City. She came to South City College five years ago to complete her Masters in Education. She started teaching Spanish here three years ago. Elena is married and has one daughter. She speaks Spanish and is planning a study trip to Mexico with her students next spring. She likes jogging and cycling. Her favorite food is pineapple. She loves teaching because she learns something new every day.

What _is_ her name. ?

When _do_ ?

Do you ?

You are , don't you?

You are , aren't you?

Did you ?

How many ?

Where ?

Why ?

Can you ?

Are you ?

?

■ STEP 3

With a partner, role-play the conversation between you and Elena Dominguez.

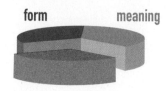

form   meaning

FOCUS 1   Review of *Yes/No* Questions

Charts.

EXAMPLES	EXPLANATIONS
(a) *Question*: Are you Brazilian? *Answer*: Yes, I am./No, I'm not. (b) *Question*: Do you understand? → *Answer*: Yes, I do./No, I don't.	When you ask a *Yes/No* question, you expect the answer *yes* or *no*. *Yes/No* questions end with rising intonation.
subject **be** (c) *Statement*: He is tired. **be** *subject* *Question*: **Is** he tired? (d) **Are** you ready to go? (e) **Am** I too late for dinner? (f) **Was** the plane on time? (g) **Were** they mad at me? *crazy.*	*Yes/No* questions with *be*: Invert the subject and the verb (move the verb **in front of** the subject).
subject *verb* (h) *Statement*: They speak Turkish. *do subject base verb* *Question*: **Do** they **speak** Turkish? (i) NOT: Speak they Turkish? (j) **Does** the bus **stop** here? (k) **Do** you **take** credit cards? (l) **Did** the President **know** about this?	*Yes/No* questions with other verbs: Put the appropriate form of *do* **in front of** the subject. Put the base form of the verb **after** the subject.
subject *be verb + -ing* (m) *Statement*: They are leaving. *be* *subject* *verb + -ing* *Question*: **Are** they **leaving**? (n) **Is** your computer **working** today? (o) **Am** I **meeting** you tomorrow? (p) **Was** it **raining** there? (q) **Were** her parents **visiting**?	*Yes/No* questions with verbs in the progressive: Invert the subject and *be* (move the *be* verb **in front of** the subject). Put the -ing form of the verb **after** the subject. For information on *Yes/No* questions with present perfect and past perfect, see Units 13–14, and 19.

EXAMPLES	EXPLANATIONS

	subject	modal	base verb
(r) Statement:	It	will	rain.

Yes/No questions with modals:
Invert the subject and the modal (put the modal **in front of** the subject). Put the base form of the verb **after** the subject.

	modal	subject	base verb
Question:	**Will**	it	**rain**?

(s) Would you repeat that?
(t) Can you help me?

(u) *Statement*: She asked him out. ➔
    Question: She asked him out? ➔
(v) You're from England?
(w) Sasha can come?
(x) He's 40 years old?
    Yes, he is.

Statement form of Yes/No questions:
A statement said with rising intonation is also a type of *Yes/No* question. This type of question is common in informal conversation.

When a statement form question is used, the speaker usually expects the listener to agree.

EXERCISE 1

Get together with a partner and make a list of five *Yes/No* questions you could ask your teacher. Write them here or in a notebook. You will have an opportunity to ask these questions later in the unit.

1. _Do you like Calgary?_

2. _Do you like to Drive a Motocycle?_

3. _Are you married?_

4. _Do you like play soccer?_

5. _Do you speack Spanish or Portuguese?_

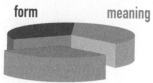

FOCUS 2   Review of *Wh*-Questions

EXAMPLES	EXPLANATIONS
(a) Q: What is your name? A: Elena. *Who What When Where* *Why Whose Which How*	A *Wh*-question usually begins with a *Wh*-word and expects the speaker to give information rather than *yes* or *no* in the answer.
(b) Where do you come from? ⟶ (c) When did you arrive? ⟶ (d) How many languages do you speak? ⟶	*Wh*-questions usually end in falling intonation.
(e) Q: Why are you late? A: Because I missed the bus. *Wh-word be subject* (f) **Where is** the restroom? (g) **What was** her name? (h) Who **are** his friends? (i) What's the time? (j) Where's my car?	**Wh-questions with *be*:** Choose a *Wh*-word. Invert the subject and the verb. In informal speech, *is* is often contracted to *'s* in *Wh*-questions.
(k) Q: When did she get here? A: Just a few minutes ago. *Wh-word do subject base verb* (l) Who(m) do you love? (m) What does a judge do? (n) Where did Nicole live?	**Wh-questions with other verbs:** Choose a *Wh*-word. To form a question, follow the *Wh*-word with a form of *do*. In informal speech, use *who* instead of *whom*.
(o) Q: What time can you leave? A: As soon as this class is over. *Wh-word modal subject base verb* (p) How long can I stay? (q) When will she come?	**Wh-questions with modals:** Choose a *Wh*-word. To form a question, put the modal directly after the *Wh*-word and before the subject.

EXERCISE 2

Get together with a partner and write down five *Wh*-questions you could ask your teacher. Write them on a piece of paper or in your notebook. You will have an opportunity to ask them later in the unit.

EXERCISE 3

Bruno and Ken are friends. Bruno has just introduced Ken to his cousin, Marta. Ken is very interested in getting to know more about her, so now he is asking Bruno all about her.

Get together with a partner and look at the answers that Bruno gave. What questions do you think Ken probably asked? Write them in the appropriate place.

Ken: (1) _____?
Bruno: Yes, I think she does.

Ken: (2) _____?
Bruno: No, she doesn't.

Ken: (3) _____?
Bruno: Usually around midnight.

Ken: (4) _____?
Bruno: Not usually.

Ken: (5) _____?
Bruno: In Buenos Aires.

Ken: (6) _____?
Bruno: Three times a week, I think.

Ken: (7) _____?
Bruno: No, she isn't.

Ken: (8) _____?
Bruno: Yes, I'm pretty sure she was.

Ken: (9) _____?
Bruno: Last year, or maybe the year before. I can't remember exactly.

Ken: (10) _____?
Bruno: I have no idea. You'll have to ask her that question yourself.

Now change partners. Read the questions that you wrote while your new partner reads Bruno's answers. When you finish, change roles to read your partner's dialogue. Compare your questions with a partner's questions. Does Marta seem like a different person? In what ways?

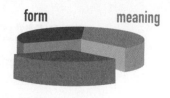

FOCUS 3 | *Wh*-Questions That Focus on the Subject

EXAMPLES	EXPLANATIONS
(a) Q: **Who(m)** did you call? A: I called Tony. *object*	This question asks about the object. *Who* is more common in informal speech. *Whom* is very formal.
(b) Q: **Who** called you? A: Martin called me. *subject*	This question asks about the subject.
Wh-word Verb (c) Q: **Who** lives here? A: Shan lives here. (d) Q: **Who** told you? A: Herb did.	For *Wh*-questions about the subject, put the appropriate *Wh*-word in front of the verb. Do not use *do* in the question.
(e) Q: **What** annoys her? A: Everything. (f) Q: **What** music annoys her? A: Rock music. (g) Q: **What** bands annoy her? A: Aerosmith and Bon Jovi.	Use *what* to ask a general question about something. Use *what* + a noun when you want a more specific answer. Make the verb singular or plural to agree with the noun.

▮ EXERCISE 4

Get together with another student or someone in your class for this exercise. First read the report on the next page. Next, think of the questions you need to ask your friend in order to complete the report. Write the questions in the "Question Box." Ask your partner all of the questions without showing them to him or her. Finally, use the answers that your friend gives you to complete the report.

Report:

My friend (1) _____ is from (2) _____ and speaks
(3) _____ languages: (4) _____. He/she was born in
(5) _____ and he/she has (6) _____ brothers and sisters.
His/her favorite subjects in school were (7) _____. He/she is taking this
class because (8) _____. In his/her free time, he/she likes to
(9) _____. His/her favorite (10) _____ is/are
(11) _____. When he/she first came here, (12) _____
surprised him/her. After he/she finishes school, he/she hopes to (13) _____.
(14) _____ make(s) him/her happy, but (15) _____ make(s)
him/her angry. Finally, there is one more thing I'd like to tell you about my friend:
(16) _____.

QUESTION BOX
1. what is your friend's name ?
2. where is is He/she from ?
3. How many languages does she/He speak ?
4. what languages does he/she speak. ?
5. where was he/she was born ?
6. How many brothes does he/she have
7. which were his/her favorite subjets? (what)
8. why does he/she take this class ?
9. what does he/she like to do in his/her free time) ?
10. Does he/she have a favorite sport ?
11. what is his/her favorite sport. ?
12. what surprised him/her when he/she first come here. ?
13. what does he/she hope to do when he/she finish class?
14. what makes he/she Happy ?
15. what makes he/she angry. ?
16. what is the last thing you'd u ? like to tell me about him/her

Chris is talking to Robin about his next vacation. Read their conversation below and write a question to go with each of Chris's answers. When you're finished, compare your questions with other students' questions in class.

Robin: (1) _what are you going_ ?
Chris: I'm going to Borneo for two weeks.

Robin: (2) _Have you been to borneo before._ ?
Chris: No, it'll be my first trip to Borneo.

Robin: (3) _what you interesting in?_ ?
Chris: The unique wildlife really interests me.

Robin: (4) _who is going with you_ ?
Chris: I'm going with two environmentalists on a study trip.

Robin: (5) _when did you met them?_ ?
Chris: I met them on a summer course last year.

Robin: (6) _what are you taking.?_ ?
Chris: We're taking backpacks and camping equipment.

what do they Have? there.

Robin: (7) _____ ?
Chris: They have some poisonous snakes there, which worries me a little.

they borneo.

Robin: (8) _when are you leaving_ ?
Chris: We're leaving on Sunday morning.

Robin: (9) _How many hours is your trip it?_
  How many hour does it take? ?
Chris: It takes twenty hours by plane.

Robin: (10) _what time is the Flight._ ?
Chris: The flight is at 4 P.M.

How much = tiempo que no se mide.
How many hours by plane?

Wh-Questions with Rising Intonation: Checking Information

use

EXAMPLES	EXPLANATIONS
(a) A: Where are you from? ➚ B: Vanuatu. (b) A: **Where** are you from? ➚ B: Vanuatu. It's in the south Pacific. (c) A: Jennifer Lopez was here last night. B: **Who** was here last night? ➚ A: Jennifer Lopez.	Most *Wh*-questions end with falling intonation. A *Wh*-question with rising intonation shows that you are not sure about what you heard or that you want to check that you heard something correctly. The *Wh*-word is also stressed (said strongly).
(d) A: Jennifer Lopez was here last night. B: **Who?** ➚	Sometimes, just the *Wh*-word (with rising intonation) is used.

EXERCISE 6

Complete the conversation with appropriate *Wh*-questions. For each question, draw an arrow ➚ or ➘ to show if the question ends with falling or rising intonation

Example: Albert: So, what did you think of the new Eisentraut movie?

Leslie: It was O.K., I guess, but I expected something more from a movie that cost $200 million to make.

Albert: (1) _____?

Leslie: $200 million. Amazing, isn't it? It's hard to imagine that amount of money.

Albert: (2) _____?

Leslie: It's an action movie set in the future, but I thought it was rather slow-moving. In fact, I almost fell asleep a couple of times.

Albert: (3) _____?

Leslie: It's about two hours, maybe a little longer. Luckily the seats were really comfortable.

Albert: (4) _____?

Leslie: At that new movie theater on Fourth Street, across from the parking garage. It only opened a couple of weeks ago, so it's got a state-of-the-art sound system, thick carpets, terrific popcorn. . . .

Albert: (5) _____?

Leslie: Twelve dollars.

Albert: (6) _____?

Leslie: Twelve dollars . . . I'm not kidding! I can't believe I spent twelve bucks on a movie that really wasn't very good.

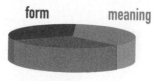
FOCUS 5   Choice Questions

EXAMPLES	EXPLANATIONS
(a) A: Are you a **graduate student or a professor?** B: I'm a graduate student. (b) A: Do you live **in a dorm or an apartment?** B: I live off campus, in an apartment.	A choice question has two or more possibilities, or options. The speaker expects you to choose one of these options in your answer. You can add more information in your answer if you want.
(c) Does Tina walk ➚ to school or take ➘ the bus? (d) A: Are you from Malaysia or from Indonesia? B: Neither. I'm from Singapore.	Choice questions have a different intonation pattern from *Yes/No* questions. *Yes/No* questions have rising intonation at the end; choice questions have rising intonation in the middle and falling intonation at the end.
(e) A: Would you like coffee or tea? B: I'll have some tea, please.	Choice questions are often used to get information quickly or to make offers (please see Unit 16 for more information on making offers with *Would . . . like*).
(f) A: (Do you want) paper or plastic? B: Paper, please.	In informal conversation, the first part of the question is sometimes dropped. Answers to choice questions are often very short. Adding *please* to your answer makes it more polite.

EXERCISE 7

Thongchai is a new student from Asia. You want to find out some information about him. Complete the following choice questions with options that are similar in meaning and form.

1. Are you from Thailand or _____?

2. Do you speak Chinese or _____?

3. Do you eat noodles or _____ for breakfast?

4. Do you live _____ or _____?

5. Are you going to study _____ or _____?

6. Do you walk to class or _____?

7. Do you like to play tennis or _____?

Practice asking and answering the questions you completed with a partner.

EXERCISE 8

Guess where each of the choice questions on the left was probably asked. Choose from the places or situations listed on the right.

QUESTIONS	PLACES/SITUATIONS
1. Paper or plastic?	A. a cash register in a department store
2. Would you like coleslaw or french fries with that?	B. a job interview
	C. a gas station
3. Do you want premium grade or regular?	D. a small shop selling hats and T-shirts
4. Will that be cash or charge?	E. an airline office
5. First class or economy?	F. a fast-food restaurant
6. Do you say "large" or "extra large"?	G. a check-out counter in a supermarket
7. Do you prefer mornings or evenings?	

Practice asking and answering the questions with a partner. Imagine yourself in each place or situation. Use more than one way of answering.

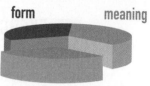

FOCUS 6   Tag Questions

EXAMPLES	EXPLANATIONS
statement **tag** (a) He is nice, **isn't he?** (b) She isn't here, **is she?** (c) We're late, **aren't we?** (d) They like it, **don't they?** (e) NOT: They like it, like they? (f) You didn't go, **did you?**	A tag question is a statement, followed by a short question (a tag). Tag questions are often used in conversation. The speaker expects a *yes* or *no* answer. The verb in the tag agrees with the subject.
statement **tag** *affirmative + negative* (g) They play tennis, **don't they?** (h) The car was hot, **wasn't it?** (i) NOT: The car was hot, was not it? (j) Our teacher will help, **won't** he? (k) She is sleeping, **isn't she?** (l) We can wait, **can't we?** (m) I am right, **aren't I?** (n) NOT: I am right, amn't I?	An affirmative statement has a negative tag. The speaker thinks that the answer will probably be *yes*. The verbs in negative tags are contracted.
statement **tag** *negative + affirmative* (o) Your friends don't drive, **do they?** (p) It wasn't hot, **was it?** (q) You won't help, **will you?** (r) The baby isn't sleeping, **is she?** (s) We can't wait, **can we?**	A negative statement has an affirmative tag. The speaker thinks that the answer will probably be *no*. The verbs in affirmative tags are not contracted.
(t) Q: You're not cold, **are you?** A: No, I'm not. (u) NOT: Yes, I'm not. (v) Q: You're cold, **aren't you?** (w) A: Yes, I am. (x) NOT: No, I am.	When you answer a tag question, respond to the statement, not to the tag. If you agree with the statement: Answer *no* to a negative statement. Answer *yes* to an affirmative statement.

EXAMPLES	EXPLANATIONS
(y) Q: She left, **didn't she**? A: (Yes,) she did. OR Right. OR I think so. (z) Q: They won't call, **will they**? A: (No,) they won't. OR I doubt it. OR Probably not. OR I don't think so. OR No way.	It's not always necessary to use the words *yes* or *no* in your answers. *No way* is very informal.

[handwritten: Don't you / Doncha.]

EXERCISE 9

Ivana is talking with her school's career counselor. Complete the counselor's questions with an appropriate tag.

1. You are studying business and computers, _aren't you_?

2. Computer skills are very important nowadays, _aren't they_?
   [handwritten crossed out: something]

3. You won't finish until next June, _will you_?

4. Your grades aren't final yet, _are they_?
   [handwritten: they]

5. You also speak Russian, _don't you_?

6. That's a difficult language, _isn't it_?

7. And you worked as a store manager in your vacations, _didn't you_?

8. You don't want to work in a large company, _do you_?

9. Those jobs can be very stressful, _can't they_?

10. But you want a job with good career opportunities, _don't you_?

11. There are a lot of different possibilities, _aren't there_?

12. We'll meet again and talk some more about it next week, _won't we_?

Deb and Sylvie are talking on the phone and making plans for their friend Bouzid's birthday.

Work with a partner. Fill in the blanks with an appropriate tag question and then put the conversation in order. Write the order of the conversation on the next page. We have done some of them for you.

DEB

B) Yes, it is, but we took him to Greens last year, _____ _____?

D) No, I won't. Maybe you should call him right away.

F) Great! I guess you don't have time to go shopping on Thursday, _____ _____?

H) Of course I will. But we'd better make sure he's free before we make any more plans.

J) Yes, he loves it. Why don't we take him to the Taj Mahal?

L) That's a great idea! And you took a class in vegetarian cooking last semester, _____ _____?

N) No, he doesn't.

P) You're right, it is. Let's take him out to a really nice restaurant.

R) No, it isn't, I forgot about that. Do you have any ideas about where to take him?

SYLVIE

A) It's Bouzid's birthday next Thursday. _____?

C) No, I don't think so. Thursdays are always so busy. But you'll be able to help me,

E) So what about Greens? Their food is all vegetarian, _____?

G) That's a good idea. He likes indian food, _____?

I) Oh my goodness, you're right, we did. So why don't we cook for him instead?

K) OK. You won't see him until the day after tomorrow, _____ _____?

M) But the Taj Mahal isn't open on Thursdays, _____?

O) I certainly did. And I've got lots of new recipes that I want to try out.

Q) Let me think... He doesn't eat meat, _____?

S) OK. I'll call him and then let you know what he says.

1. __A__   4. ____   7. ____   10. ____   13. ____   16. ____   18. ____
2. __P__   5. ____   8. ____   11. ——   14. ____   17. ____   19. __S__
3. __G__   6. ____   9. __E__   12. ____   15. ____

You can find the answers to this exercise on page A-15.

use

FOCUS 7	Tag Question Intonation

EXAMPLES

(a) Q: His name is Tom, isn't it?
    A: Yes, it is.

(b) Q: It's not going to rain today, is it?
    A: No, it isn't.

(c) Q: His name is Tom, isn't it?
(d) Q: It's not going to rain today, is it?

EXPLANATIONS

Falling intonation in tag questions shows that the speaker is fairly sure that the information in the statement is true. The speaker is also sure that the listener will agree.

A person making an affirmative statement with falling intonation (a) expects the answer *yes*. A person making a negative statement with falling intonation (b) expects the answer *no*.

Rising intonation in tag questions shows that the speaker is not sure if the information in the statement is true.

EXERCISE 11

Go back to the conversation in Exercise 10. With a partner, draw arrows ⟋ or ⟍ to show falling or rising intonation in the tags. One of you will take Sylvie's part and the other will take Deb's. Read the exercise aloud to practice intonation. Finally, get together with another pair and listen to each other's performances.

EXERCISE 12

Your teacher will ask some tag questions. Circle **Y** if you think the expected answer is **yes** and **N** if you think the expected answer is **no**.

1. Y   N   4. Y   N   7. Y   N
2. Y   N   5. Y   N   8. Y   N
3. Y   N   6. Y   N   9. Y   N

EXERCISE 13

Read each tag question aloud, using the intonation as marked. For each question, tell whether the speaker expects a certain answer, and if so, what the speaker expects the answer to be, *yes* or *no*. Answer the question the way you think the speaker expects it to be answered.

	(a) Is the speaker fairly sure what the answer will be?	(b) If *yes* to (a), answer the question.
1. It's going to rain today, isn't it? ➞		
2. You don't know where my umbrella is, do you? ➞		
3. You're driving today, aren't you? ➞		
4. It's not my turn to drive, is it? ➞		
5. You made lunch for me, didn't you? ➞		
6. I didn't forget to thank you, did I? ➞		
7. I'm pretty forgetful, aren't I? ➞		

EXERCISE 14

Your teacher has been nominated for a "Teacher-of-the-Year Award" and will appear at a press conference to answer questions from journalists and reporters. You and your classmates are all newspaper reporters. You need to write a profile of your teacher for your paper and want to get as much information from him or her as possible.

STEP 1   Get together with two or three other students. As a group, choose eight questions that you would most like to ask your teacher at the press conference. You can use some of the questions you wrote in Exercise 1, Exercise 2, and the Opening Task if you want to, or you can make completely new questions. Important note:

- Two questions must be *Yes/No* questions.
- Two questions must be *Wh*-questions.
- Two questions must be *tag* questions.
- Two questions must be choice questions.

STEP 2   When you have decided on your questions, your teacher will hold the press conference, but he or she will only answer your questions if they are correctly formed and if the intonation is appropriate. If another group asks a question that your group wanted to ask, you must ask a different question (your teacher will not answer the same question twice). Write your questions and the answers below. If possible, record the "press conference" and listen to the recording to check your intonation and your teacher's answers.

QUESTIONS	ANSWERS

Use Your English

ACTIVITY 1 speaking/listening

■ **STEP 1**   Your teacher is going to stick a piece of paper on your back and on the backs of your classmates. Get up and walk around the class, looking at what is written on your classmates' backs.

■ **STEP 2**   Your job is to guess what is written on your back. You can find this out by asking questions. You can also answer the questions that your classmates ask you about what is written on their backs. For the first five minutes, you can only ask *Yes/No* questions. Refuse to answer any question that is not a *Yes/No* question. When your teacher gives you a signal, you can ask any kind of question that you like. Here are some possible *Yes/No* questions to ask: Is this a person? Is this person male or female? Is this an object? Is it expensive? Is this an animal? Is this food? Here are some possible *Wh*-questions: How big is this? Where was he or she born? What color is this?

ACTIVITY 2 speaking/writing

The international student office at your school is preparing a short guide for students who have just arrived in this country. The purpose of this guide is to give new students a clear idea of what to expect when they arrive here. You have been asked to write a chapter called "Frequently asked questions."

Get together with two or three other students and make a list of all the questions that people in this country frequently ask you. Compare your lists with those of other students in the class. Use the information from your classmates to make a list of the questions that people here frequently ask international students and that new students should be ready to answer.

ACTIVITY 3 speaking/writing

Work in a group. You are going to play the role of career counselor to one person in your group. Make a list of 10–15 questions that would help that person decide what kind of career to choose. Write the questions on a sheet of paper. When you are ready, choose one person to answer your questions (you can add further questions during the interview!). Then change roles.

ACTIVITY 4 writing/reading

■ STEP 1

In this activity you cannot speak, but you can write. Sit down next to a student that you do not know very well. Spend a couple of minutes thinking about some of the things you would like to know about this person. Take a piece of paper and write **one** question for your partner to answer. Pass the question to your partner. Read the question that your partner gives you. Without speaking, write your answer to the question and write another question for your partner to answer. **Do not speak at all**.

■ STEP 2

Exchange papers with your partner. Read your partner's answer to your question and answer his or her question to you. Continue writing questions and answers to each other until your teacher tells you to stop. Now you can speak!

Optional: With your partner's permission, share some of the information from your silent interview with the rest of the class.

■ STEP 3

Look back over the questions that you and your partner wrote. Were you able to use any of the kinds of questions discussed in this unit?

ACTIVITY 5 speaking/listening

Your English teacher has just quit her job and is now relaxing on a beach in Tahiti. Your school is desperately searching for a new teacher. Your classmates have decided to take matters into their own hands and you have decided to interview teachers yourselves. Pretend one of your classmates is an applicant for the position. Ask him or her some questions about his or her experience, interests, and future goals. Listen to your classmate's answers. They may help you ask other questions.

ACTIVITY 6 listening/writing

CD Tracks
6,7

A friend of yours has applied for a job teaching English in Latvia. She cannot travel to Latvia for a job interview, so the school has to interview her by phone. You are at her house when the school calls. You can hear her half of the conversation (the answers that she gives), but you can't hear the questions that the interviewer asked.

Listen to your friend's half of the conversation. In the first column, write the questions that you think the interviewer **probably** asked. Then listen to the complete interview to compare your questions with the ones the interviewer **actually** asked. Use the second column to write any questions that are different from the ones in the first column.

PROBABLE QUESTIONS	ACTUAL QUESTIONS

ACTIVITY 7   speaking/writing

Imagine you are going to write an essay on one of these topics: (1) Learning a foreign language, (2) Applying for a job, or (3) Using the Internet for research.

What three main questions will your essay answer? Compare your questions with another student. Write your questions on the board and choose the best three for each title.

ACTIVITY 8   speaking/listening

Bring in a photograph and give it to your teacher. Your teacher will mix up the pictures and distribute them randomly. Look at your photograph for thirty seconds and then give it back to the teacher. The teacher will put all the photographs on a table or hang them up. Students will take turns being questioned by the class. When it is your turn, your classmates will ask you questions about the picture you looked at. They will try to guess which picture it was. Try to use all types of questions: *Yes/No*, *Wh-*, statement form, choice, and tag.

ACTIVITY 9   research on the web

InfoTrac® College Edition: Go to *InfoTrac* to find information about a country you are interested in. Type in the name of the country and *Fact File*, for example, *France Fact File*. Make a list of questions using information in the article. Ask your classmates if they know the answers.

ACTIVITY 10   reflection

Work in a group. Choose one aspect of learning English, for example, writing or vocabulary. Write a questionnaire about how students in your class learn and practice this skill. Interview other students in your class using your questionnaire. Report the results to the class. What general patterns did you find?

5

MODALS OF PROBABILITY AND POSSIBILITY

Could, May, Might, Must, Couldn't, and *Can't*

UNIT GOALS

- Use *could, may, might, must, couldn't,* and *can't* to show how certain you are about a present situation

- Form statements and questions to describe probability and possibility in the present and past

- Use the progressive with modals of probability and possibility

- Use *could, may, might, will/be (probably) going to, may not,* and *might not* to talk about future probability and possibility

OPENING TASK

Identify the Mystery Person

One evening toward the end of March, a New York taxi driver found that someone had left a briefcase on the back seat of his cab. When he opened it, he found that the briefcase was empty, except for the things you can see on the next page.

■ STEP 1

With a partner, examine everything on the next page carefully. Can you find any clues about the identity of the owner of the briefcase? Use the chart to write down your ideas and to show how certain you are about them.

HOW CERTAIN ARE YOU?	GUESSES										
	Name	Sex	Age	Marital Status	Occupation	Likes and Interests	Family and Friends	Habits	Recent Activities	Future Plans	Anything else?
Less than 50% certain (it's possible)			46								.
90% certain (it's probable)	Men				businessman			Parties	Business Meeting	trip to Japan	He/she works to much.
100% certain (it's certain)	Chris Murray			Married		Sports and art	He/she has a family.				

MARCH

SUNDAY	MONDAY	TUESDAY	WEDNESDAY	THURSDAY	FRIDAY	SATURDAY
1	2 Board meeting 10:30 send papers to Washington	3 meeting 8 lunch Sally leave for NYC 7:00	4 Ash Wednesday NYC EXECUTIVE MEETING	5	6 return from NYC meeting 10:30 drinks Bob Theatre 8:30	7 wedding anniversary dinner 8
8 golf 9:30	9 report on NYC meeting due	10 Sally's Birthday meeting with Vice president 2.p.m. movie 8	11 Paris meeting arrive 14.50	12	13	14 Call Sally
15 Purim	16 Accountant Lunch Robert Haywood Call Paris Office	17 St. Patrick's Day Opera 9:30	18 Visitors from Tokyo office Dinner Japanese restaurant 7p.m.	19	20 Export meeting	21 Spring Begins tennis 2p.m. Mike Kids home from school
22 golf 9:30	23 Japanese Class	24 Doctor: 8 sales meeting 10:30	25 9:00 Accountant tennis Mike	26 Lunch SALLY	27 Doctor: 9 10:00 sales meeting Japanese Class	28 check passport
29 TOKYO?	30	31				

STEP 2

Now get together with a group and share your ideas about the identity of this mystery person, showing how certain you feel about each one.

Example: *He might be a businessman.*

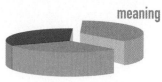

FOCUS 1

Using *Could, Might, May, Must, Couldn't,* and *Can't* to Show How Certain You Are about the Present

EXAMPLES	EXPLANATIONS
	Could, might, may, and *must* show how certain or not you are about a present situation.
Situation: He's got a baseball hat on. *Less Certain* ▲ (a) He could play baseball. │ (b) He might play baseball. ▼ (c) He may play baseball. *More Certain*	**Possible (less than 50% certain)** Use *could, might,* or *may* to express possibility (to show that you believe something is possible, but you are not very certain if it is true or not). You are making a guess. *May* shows that you are a little more certain that something is true.
Situation: She is wearing a white coat. *Less Certain* ▲ (d) She **could** be a doctor. │ (e) She **might** be a doctor. ▼ (f) She **may** be a doctor. *More Certain*	

Situation: He's wearing a baseball hat.
He's carrying a baseball glove.
    (g) He **must** play baseball.
 	
Situation: She is carrying a stethoscope.
    (h) She **must** be a doctor.
	Probable (about 90% certain)
	Use *must* to express probability (to show that you believe something is probably true).
	
	You are **almost** certain that this is true. You are drawing a conclusion, based on what you know.

(i) He **couldn't** be a soccer player. (j) She **can't** be a teacher.	Use *couldn't* and *can't* to show that you are almost certain that something is **not** true.

Situation: It's the middle of a baseball game.
He is throwing a ball to his teammate.
    (k) He **plays** baseball.
 	
Situation: She performed heart surgery on my mother in the hospital and saved her life.
    (l) She **is** a doctor.
    (m) She **isn't** a nurse.
	Certain (100% certain)
	These are facts. You are completely certain about these situations. Do not use *could, might, may,* or *must.*
	
	For information on other ways of using *could, might, may,* and *must,* see Units 10, 11, and 17.

EXERCISE 1

Look at the situations below and complete the sentences to show how certain the speaker is about each one.

SITUATION	POSSIBLE
She always wears a purple hat.	**Less Certain** ↑ 1. She _____ like purple. ↓ 2. She _____ like purple. 3. She _____ like purple. *More Certain*
Situation	Probable
She always wears a purple hat and a purple coat.	4. She _____ like purple.
Situation	Certain
She always wears purple clothes, she drives a purple car, and lives in a purple house surrounded by purple flowers.	5. She _____ purple.
Situation	Possible
He's carrying a French newspaper.	**Less Certain** ↑ 6. He _____ be French. ↓ 7. He _____ be French. 8. He _____ be French. *More Certain*
Situation	Probable
He's carrying a French newspaper and he's speaking French to the people with him.	9. He _____ be French.
Situation	Certain
He's carrying a French newspaper and he's speaking French to the people with him. He was born in France and has a French passport.	10. He _____ be British. 11. He _____ be French.

Compare your answers with a partner's and then check what you have written with the information in Focus 1.

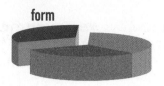
form

FOCUS 2 Modals of Probability and Possibility

EXAMPLES	EXPLANATIONS
subject + modal + verb (a) Jack **could** live here. (b) NOT: Jack could lives here. (c) Alex **might** know him. (d) NOT: Alex mights know him. (e) Shirley **may** be at home. (f) NOT: Shirley maybe at home.	**Affirmative Statements** Modals come before the base form of the verb. Modals have only one form. They do not take *s*. *Maybe* is not a modal.
subject + modal + not + verb (g) She **must not** like cats. (h) Bo **might not** know that. (i) That's impossible! Ron **couldn't** be in Las Vegas. I saw him just a few minutes ago. He **can't** be there.	**Negative Statements** *May not, might not,* and *must not* are not usually contracted when they express possibility or probability. *Couldn't/can't* show that you strongly believe that something is impossible. *Couldn't/can't* are usually contracted. However, *could* expresses very weak certainty. It shows that you are not very certain if something is possible.
modal + subject + verb (k) **Could** Sid be in Reno? (l) **Might** Cathy know about this?	**Questions** *May* and *must* are not used in questions about possibility and probability.

Question: *Answer:*
(m) Does he take   I'm not sure.
   the train?   He **might**.
(n) Does Sue like   She **may not**.
   Thai food?   She doesn't like spicy food very much.
 	
(o) Is Jay at home?   He **might be**. He's not in his office.
(p) Is Tom busy right   He **might not be**. I'll now?   ask him.
	Short Answers
	Use the modal by itself in short answers.
	
	Use the modal + *be* in short answers to questions with *be*.
	Use the modal + *not* for negative short answers.

EXERCISE 2

Turn back to the Opening Task on pages 70–71. Make statements about the owner of the briefcase. Use *must, may, could, might, couldn't,* or *can't* to show how certain you feel. Share your opinions with your classmates and be ready to justify them as necessary.

Example: **Name:** *In my opinion, the owner of the briefcase might be called Chris Murray because this name is on the boarding pass. However, this boarding pass could belong to somebody else.*

1. SEX: In my opinion, the owner of the briefcase *must be a men,* because *his name is chris, and He likes sports.*

2. OCCUPATION: I believe he or she *must be a businessperson* because, *he or she has a lot of trips an meeting.*

3. MARITAL STATUS: This person *is marries* I think this because *He/She has in his/her schedule has the day of the aniversary.*

4. LIKES AND INTERESTS: *He/She is intresting in sports and Arts.*

5. HABITS: *He/She must be intresting in business and make money.*

6. AGE: *He/She could be 46 years old*

EXERCISE 3

Add an appropriate short answer to the questions in these conversations. The first one has been done for you. Several responses are possible.

A: Where's Mike? Is he at lunch?

B: I don't know. He (1) _____ might be. _____

A: Do you know if he speaks Turkish?

B: Yes, he (2) _____ does _____. He lived in Turkey for ten years. ✓

A: Do you think he has time to help me translate this letter?

B: I'm not sure. He (3) _____ couldn't _____ (not). He'll be in meetings all day today.
may not
might not

A: Do you know if he'll come back here later?

B: He (4) _____ could _____, but I don't really know.
may

A: Will he be here tomorrow?

B: He (5) _____ couldn't _____ (not). I think he is planning to work at home tomorrow.
can't

A: If I leave message, will he call me? It's very urgent.

B: Well, he (6) _____ may _____, but I can't say for sure.
could

form

FOCUS 3	Modals of Probability and Possibility in the Past

EXAMPLES	EXPLANATIONS
subject + modal + have + past participle (a) Vi **may have left.** (b) I'm not sure how Liz went home last night. She **could have taken** a cab. (c) There's nobody here; everyone **must have gone** out.	**Affirmative Statements** Choose the appropriate modal + *have* + past participle to show how certain you are about something that happened in the past.
subject + modal + not + have + past participle (d) I **may not have seen** him. (e) Selena **might not have been** in town last week. (f) Darius **couldn't have robbed** the store. He was at home with me all evening.	**Negative Statements:** Choose the appropriate modal + *not* + *have* + past participle to show how certain you are that something did **not** happen in the past.
modal + subject + have + past participle? (g) **Could** she **have known?** (h) **Might** the police **have followed** the stolen car?	**Questions:** Choose the appropriate modal + subject + *have* + past participle to ask about possibility and probability in the past. Remember that *must* and *may* are not usually used in questions about possibility or probability.
(i) Q: Did Jerry talk to Kramer last night? A: I'm not sure. He **may have.** (j) Q: Did Bernadette remember to go to the store? A: She **must have.** The refrigerator is full of food.	**Short Answers:** Use the appropriate modal + *have* in short answers.
(k) Q: Was Vinny depressed? A: It's hard to say. He **might have been.** (l) NOT: He might have.	Remember to use the appropriate modal + *have been* in short answers to questions using *be*.

EXERCISE 4

Turn back to the Opening Task. Make statements showing how certain you are about the person's past activities. Use *must, may, could, might, couldn't,* or *can't* + *have* + past participle to show how certain you feel. Be ready to share and justify your opinions.

EXERCISE 5

Read the following situations. Can you figure out what happened? Think of as many possible explanations as you can. Then compare your ideas with a partner.

Example: You are walking along the street when you see a $20 bill on the ground.
Someone must have dropped it. Someone might have put it there as a trick.

1. A boy is crawling on the ground looking for something. He is crying.
   He could have lost his Toy.   He may have a pain.

2. A car has stopped in the middle of the road. A bicycle is on the ground next to the car.
   It could be broken /   The cars may have been weating for the bicycle

3. There is a big hole in the front window of the bank. *the bank could*
   A men could have been stealing /   have been stealing.

4. Your train is twenty minutes late.
   I could have been late /   the train must be broke.

5. A man and a woman are sitting in a restaurant. The woman is holding a diamond ring. She looks surprised.
   He must have proposed /   she may has been answering.

6. A man is standing outside a house. He is wearing pajamas and slippers. He is holding a newspaper and ringing the front door bell.
   He could have been lost /   He may be ringing the bell.

7. A man is standing in line at the bus stop. His coat is completely wet.
   It could have been raining
   Someone may have beeen splashing.

splash

form

FOCUS 4 — Modals of Probability and Possibility with the Progressive

EXAMPLES	EXPLANATIONS
subject + modal + be + verb + -ing (a) He **might be sleeping.** (b) Q: What's Lisa doing these days? A: I'm really not sure. She **may be working** in Latvia. (c) Something smells good! Albert **must be cooking** dinner. (d) You **must know** the Van Billiard family. They live in Amherst. (e) NOT: You must be knowing the Van Billiard family.	Use modals with the progressive to make a guess or draw a conclusion about something in progress at or around the time of speaking. Remember that some verbs cannot be used in the progressive. For more information, see Unit 2.
subject + modal + have been + verb + -ing (f) He **may have been sleeping**. (g) Mo **must have been working** on his car; his hands are really dirty.	Use this form to make a guess or draw a conclusion about something that was in progress before the time of speaking.

EXERCISE 6

Look back at the situations in Exercise 5. Can you make any statements about the people in these situations using _must, may, might,_ or _could_ with a progressive form? Use present forms (to talk about what you think they might be doing now) or past forms (to talk about what you think they might have been doing before now). For example: _Someone may be watching to see how many people try to pick up the $20 bill._ Compare your ideas with a partner's.

EXERCISE 7

The police are investigating a murder. What might Sherlock Holmes conclude about the following pieces of evidence? Get together with a partner to come up with a theory about what happened. After that, share your conclusions with the rest of the class, using *must, may, could, might*, or *couldn't/can't* to show how certain you feel. Finally, take a vote to decide who has the most interesting theory. How probable do you think this theory is?

Police Report:

The victim was found in her bedroom on the second floor of her house. The front door and her bedroom door were locked from inside. There were two wine glasses on the table in her room; one was empty, the other was full. There was an ashtray with several cigarette butts in it. The victim had a small white button in her hand and several long, blond hairs. Her watch was found on the floor; it had stopped at 11:30. The drawers of the victim's desk were open, and there were papers all over the floor. Nothing appeared to be missing.

EXERCISE 8

You are a reporter for your local newspaper. The editor has asked you to report on the murder described in Exercise 7. Explain what you think happened and why you believe this to be so. Make a headline for your report. Display your headline and your report so that your classmates can compare the different theories about the murder.

FOCUS 5	Future Probability and Possibility with Modals

EXAMPLES	EXPLANATIONS
(a) There are a few clouds in the sky; it **could** **might** **may** rain later. (b) Cheer up! She **might** call tomorrow. (c) We **may** see them next month.	Use *could, might,* or *may* to express future possibility. *May* shows that you are a little more certain that something will happen.
(d) Q: Where's Anna? A: She'll **probably** get here soon. (e) NOT: She must get here soon. (f) Q: What's Jim going to do after he graduates next year? A: He's **probably going to** travel around the world on a motorcycle. (g) NOT: He must travel round the world on a motorcycle.	Use *will* or *be going to* with *probably* to show that you are almost certain that something will happen in the future. Do not use *must.*
(h) Look! The sun's coming out. It **may not** rain after all. (i) NOT: It could not rain after all. (j) Fran **might not** come to the airport with us tomorrow. (k) NOT: Fran could not come to the airport with us tomorrow.	Use *may not* or *might not* to show that it is possible that something will **not** happen. Do not use *could not.*

EXERCISE 9

Work with a partner and turn back to the Opening Task. From the evidence given, what can you say about the person's future plans? Use *probably will/be going to, may, could, must,* or *may not/might not* as necessary. Be prepared to share and justify your answers.

Work with a partner and choose the best way to complete each sentence. Bubble in the correct answer. Discuss the reasons for your choice. Share your reasons with the rest of the class.

1. **A:** Where's Rose?
   B: I'm not sure. She _____ in the library.
   ○ *is*   ○ *might be*   ○ *must be*

2. **A:** My daughter just got a scholarship to Stanford!
   B: You _____ be very proud of her.
   ○ *could*   ○ *must*   ○ *might*

3. **A:** How does Sheila get to school?
   B: I don't really know. She _____ the bus.
   ○ *might take*   ○ *takes*   ○ *must take*

4. **A:** It's really cold in here today
   B: Yes. Somebody _____ the window open.
   ○ *must leave*   ○ *might leave*   ○ *must have left*

5. **A:** I wonder why Zelda always wears gloves.
   B: I don't know. She _____ some kind of allergy.
   ○ *may have had*   ○ *has*   ○ *may have*

6. **A:** Have you heard the weather forecast?
   B: No, but look at all those dark clouds in the sky. I think it _____ rain.
   ○ *could*   ○ *must*   ○ *is probably going to*

7. **A:** Did my mother call while I was out?
   B: I'm not sure. She _____.
   ○ *might have*   ○ *might*   ○ *did*

8. **A:** Ellen gave a violin recital in front of five hundred people yesterday. It was her first public performance.
   B: Really? She _____ very nervous.
   ○ *could have been*   ○ *must be*   ○ *must have been*

9. **A:** Are you coming to Jeff's party?
   B: I'm not sure. I _____ go to the concert instead.
   ○ *must*   ○ *will*   ○ *might*

10. **A:** Can I speak to Professor Carroll?
    B: She's not in her office, and she doesn't have any more classes today, so she _____ home.
    ○ *might go*   ○ *must have gone*   ○ *will probably go*

11. **A:** Jenny's sneezing again.

    B: Yes, she _____ a terrible cold.

    ○ *must have*   ○ *must be having*   ○ *must have had*

12. **A:** Look, Maynard's sitting outside his own apartment. Isn't that weird?

    B: Not really. He _____ his keys, and now he's waiting for his wife to come home.

    ○ *may be losing*   ○ *may have lost*   ○ *may have been losing*

13. **A:** Is Myrna working in the city today?

    B: She _____. I'm not sure.

    ○ *could*   ○ *could have*   ○ *could be*

14. **A:** I can hear the water running in the bathroom.

    B: Yes, Bira _____ another shower.

    ○ *must take*   ○ *must have taken*   ○ *must be taking*

15. **A:** What's up? You look worried.

    B: I am. My dog's sick. I think he _____ eaten some poison.

    ○ *may be*   ○ *may have been*   ○ *may have*

16. **A:** Have you heard? Mel's father died last night.

    B: Poor Mel. He _____ feeling terrible. They were very close.

    ○ *must*   ○ *must be*   ○ *must have been*

17. **A:** Dean has just won a million dollars in the lottery.

    B: He _____. He never buys lottery tickets.

    ○ *must not have*   ○ *could not*   ○ *couldn't have*

18. **A:** Does Isaiah still share a house with his sister?

    B: I don't know. He _____.

    ○ *might be*   ○ *might*   ○ *might have*

EXERCISE 11

Look back at the Opening Task. Who do you think the "Mystery Person" is? What do you think happened to him or her? Complete the following newspaper article with your ideas about what might have happened. Remember to use *must, may, could, might*, or *couldn't/can't* to show how certain you feel.

MISSING MYSTERY PERSON

It has been a week since New York taxi driver Ricardo Oliveiro found a briefcase on the back seat of his cab. It has been a week of guessing and speculation: Who is the owner of this briefcase and where is he or she now? Several different theories have been proposed, but so far the most interesting is the one which follows . . .

Use Your English

ACTIVITY 1 speaking/listening

Can you guess these objects? Get together with a partner and see how many different possibilities you can come up with for each picture. Classify your interpretations as "Possible," "Probable," and "Certain." Compare your answers with the rest of the class. (You can find the answers on page A-15.)

It could be a jirafe

 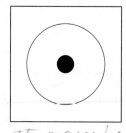 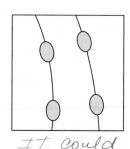

It many be a CD.   *It could be a planet.*

ACTIVITY 2 speaking/listening

■ STEP 1 The purpose of this activity is to confuse your classmates. Form teams and create five different drawings of familiar things seen from an unusual point of view. One example is shown below.

■ STEP 2 Exchange papers with another team. As a team, see how many different interpretations you can make of each drawing. Write each guess beside the appropriate drawing, showing how probable you think your interpretation is.

■ STEP 3 When you have made your guesses, exchange papers with another team until all teams have had a chance to "interpret" all the drawings.

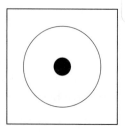

It could be a donut.
It might be a hat from above.
It could be an eyeball.

Which team got the most "correct" interpretations? Which team had the most interesting or unusual interpretations?

Get together with a partner and examine the pictures below. What's going on? Who are the people? Imagine this story happened yesterday. Create a newspaper story telling what you think might have happened. You can use the photographs in any order that you like. Compare your story with those of your classmates. In what ways do their interpretations differ from yours?

ACTIVITY 4 listening

CD Track 8

■ **STEP 1**
Listen to the audio of two different people talking about the pictures on page 85. As you listen to their stories, number each picture to show which one comes first, second, and so on. Which story is the most likely, in your opinion? Speaker 1's story or Speaker 2's story?

■ **STEP 2**
Listen to the audio again and write any sentences with *may, might, could,* or *must* that show how certain the speaker feels.

ACTIVITY 5 speaking/listening

■ **STEP 1**
Look at the pictures below. What events are going to happen in each picture? What are you certain will happen? What is possibly going to happen? What are you not sure about?

■ **STEP 2**
Show the pictures to a friend. Ask him or her to tell you what he or she thinks might happen next. Take notes or record the answers he or she gives. Review your notes or listen to your recording and make notes. Do students have different ideas about the photos? Which ones are the most interesting? Tell your classmates.

ACTIVITY 6 speaking/listening

In the Opening Task, you looked at the contents of somebody's briefcase and made guesses about his or her identity. The purpose of this activity is to create your own "mystery person." Form groups and collect a number of items that somebody might carry in his or her pockets (tickets, bills, photographs, business cards, etc.). Choose six items, collect them in a bag, and bring them to class. Exchange bags with another group. With your group, examine the contents of the new bag and try to decide on the possible identity of the owner, using the same categories as in the Opening Task. When everyone is ready, share your conclusions with the rest of the class, showing how certain you are. Remember, your classmates might ask you to justify your conclusions, so be ready to justify each one.

ACTIVITY 7 writing

Write a profile of the "mystery person" your group presented to the class in Activity 6. Make sure you write an introductory sentence and that you provide evidence to support your conclusions. When you finish writing, read your profile to see how much of the language discussed in this unit you were able to use.

ACTIVITY 8 research on the web

On the Web: Look up one of these mysteries on the Internet using a search engine such as Google® or Yahoo® and make notes about what happened: 1) Stonehenge 2) the statues of Rapa Nui 3) the Mayan civilization. What is mysterious about them? Tell your classmates and ask them for suggestions about what might/may/could have happened.

ACTIVITY 9 reflection

Make a list of five things to do before taking an exam. Say what may/might/could happen if you don't follow this advice.

Example: *Don't stay up late the night before an exam, otherwise you might feel tired or sleepy during the exam.*

PAST PROGRESSIVE AND SIMPLE PAST WITH TIME CLAUSES
When, While, and *As Soon As*

UNIT GOALS

- Choose between past progressive and simple past

- Form past progressive correctly

- Understand the meaning of *when, while,* and *as soon as*

- Form clauses with *when, while,* and *as soon as*

OPENING TASK
Miami Murder Mystery

Last night Lewis Meyer died at his home in Miami. Phil Fork, a police detective, was the first person to arrive at the house after Mr. Meyer died. This is what he found:

Mr. Meyer's wife, Margo, told Fork: "It was an accident. My husband took a shower at about 10:00 P.M. After his shower, he slipped on a piece of soap and fell down."

theory

Do you believe her? What probably happened?

Look at the picture and work with a partner. Decide whether the following statements are **probably** true (T) or **probably** false (F). Be ready to share your answers with your classmates and to explain your choices.

1. Mr. Meyer died after Phil Fork arrived. (T) F
2. Mr. Meyer died when Phil Fork arrived. T (F)
3. Mr. Meyer died before Phil Fork arrived. (T) F
4. Mr. Meyer brushed his teeth before he died. T (F)
5. Mr. Meyer was brushing his teeth when he died. (T) F
6. Mr. Meyer was taking a shower when he died. T (F)
7. Mr. Meyer took a shower before he died. (T) F
8. Mr. Meyer died when he slipped on a piece of soap. (T) F
9. Somebody hit Mr. Meyer over the head while he was brushing his teeth. (T) F
10. The murder (weapon) is still in the bathroom. (T) F

You are the detective. In your opinion, how did Mr. Meyer die?

With your partner, use the picture and your answers above to try to solve the mystery. Make as many guesses as you like. For example: *We think somebody killed Mr. Meyer while he was brushing his teeth. This is how it happened.* . . . Be ready to share your ideas with the rest of the class. Write your ideas here:

WHAT REALLY HAPPENED:

① while Mr Meyer was brushing his teeth, his wife put the soap on the floor.
③ when he turned around, he slipped and fall on the floor...
② Mr. Meyer was deciding to return to the shower to pick up his towel.

(Solution to the Opening Task on page A-15)

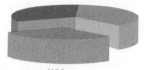

FOCUS 1 — Past Progressive and Simple Past

use

EXAMPLES	EXPLANATIONS
(a) Phil Fork **arrived** at 10:30. (b) Mrs. Meyer **drank** several cups of black coffee.	Use the simple past for an action that started and finished in the past. For a list of irregular past forms, see Appendix 5 on page A-13.
(c) Phil Fork **was eating** dinner at 10:00. (d) Mr. Meyer **was brushing** his teeth at 10:00	*Was eating* and *was brushing* are past progressive. Use the past progressive for an action that was in progress at a specific time in the past.
(e) Mr. Meyer **was brushing** his teeth when the murderer **entered** the room. (f) Phil Fork **was eating** dinner when he heard about the murder.	Use the past progressive with the simple past to show that one action began first and was still in progress when the second action happened. It is possible that the first action continued after the second action finished.
(g) Mrs. Meyer **was talking** on the phone while her husband **was taking** a shower. (h) Phil Fork **was reading** a newspaper while he **was eating** dinner.	Use the past progressive with the past progressive to show two actions in progress at the same time.

EXERCISE 1

Look back at what you wrote in the Opening Task on page 89. Did you use the past progressive and the simple past? If you did, <u>underline</u> all of your examples of the past progressive, circle all examples of the simple past, and check with your teacher to see if you used them correctly. If you didn't use these forms at all, write three sentences about Mr. Meyer's murder using the past progressive and the simple past. Check with your teacher to see if you used these forms correctly.

1. _____

2. _____

3. _____

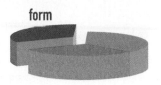

FOCUS 2   Past Progressive

STATEMENT	NEGATIVE	QUESTION
I She He It } was sleeping.	I She He It } was not sleeping. (wasn't)	Was { I she he it } sleeping?
We You They } were sleeping.	We You They } were not sleeping. (weren't)	Were { we you they } sleeping?

EXERCISE 2

Get together with a partner and complete this newspaper report of Mr. Meyer's murder. Use information from the Opening Task on page 88 and your own ideas about what happened to help you.

DAILY NEWS

BATHROOM MURDER

"I am innocent!" says Mrs. Meyer.

Last night police arrested Margo Meyer for the murder of her husband, Lewis. On her way to the police station, Mrs. Meyer told reporters: "I am innocent. I loved my husband very much. I didn't kill him."

According to Mrs. Meyer, on the night of his death, her husband _____

_____ when

_____ .

However, Detective Phil Fork and his colleagues have a different theory about how Mr. Meyer died. According to them, _____

_____

_____ while _____

_____ .

meaning

FOCUS 3 | *When, While,* and *As Soon As*

EXAMPLES	EXPLANATIONS
(a) **While** Mr. Meyer was getting ready for bed, Mrs. Meyer drank several cups of black coffee. OR (b) Mrs. Meyer drank several cups of black coffee **while** Mr. Meyer was getting ready for bed.	*When, while,* and *as soon as* give information about time. You can use them **either** at the beginning of a sentence **or** in the middle. *While* introduces an action in progress. It means "during that time." It is usually used with the past progressive.
(c) Mrs. Meyer called the police **when** she found the dead body. OR (d) **When** Mrs. Meyer found her husband's body, she called the police.	*When* introduces a completed action. It is usually used with the simple past. In (c) and (d), *when* introduces the action that happened first: **First** Mrs. Meyer found the body and **then** she called the police.
(e) Mrs. Meyer came to the door **as soon as** Phil Fork arrived. OR (f) **As soon as** Phil Fork arrived, Mrs. Meyer came to the door.	*As soon as* introduces a completed action and means "immediately after."

Make meaningful statements about Mr. Meyer's murder by matching information from A with information from B. The first one has been done for you.

A	B
1. Mrs. Meyer called the police	she said that she was innocent.
2. While she was waiting for the police to arrive	Mrs. Meyer took him to the scene of the crime.
3. As soon as Phil Fork heard about the murder	as soon as her husband died.
4. When Fork asked to see the body	while the police were taking her to jail.
5. While Fork was searching the bathroom for clues	while he was brushing his teeth.
6. He saw that Mr. Meyer died	she placed a bar of soap on the bathroom floor.
7. When Fork accused Mrs. Meyer of murder.	he rushed to the Meyers' house.
8. A crowd of news reporters tried to interview Mrs. Meyer	he became suspicious of Mrs. Meyer's story.

EXERCISE 4

Look again at the sentences you created in Exercise 3. For each one, underline the part of the sentence that gives information about time. This is the part of the sentence that answers the question "When?"

Example: *Mrs. Meyer called the police <u>as soon as</u> her husband died.*

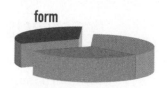

form

FOCUS 4

Time Clauses with *When, While, As Soon As, Before,* and *After*

EXAMPLES	EXPLANATIONS

EXAMPLES

Dependent Time Clause	*Main Independent Clause*

(a)
When Amy returned home,   everyone ran out to greet her.

(b) While my father was cooking dinner, our guests arrived.

(c) Our guests arrived while my father was cooking dinner.

EXPLANATIONS

A time clause is a **dependent** clause; this means that it is not complete by itself. It needs the rest of the sentence (**the main or independent** clause) to complete its meaning.

In order to understand *When Amy returned home,* we need more information.

A time clause can come at the beginning of a sentence (b) **or** at the end (c). If the time clause comes at the beginning of the sentence, use a comma between the time clause and the main clause.

When ~~~~~~~~, ~~~~~~~~

If the main clause comes at the beginning of the sentence and the time clause comes last, do not use a comma between the two clauses (c).

~~ **when** ~~~~~~~~

EXERCISE 5

Turn back to the sentences you created in Exercise 3. Write them below and add commas, as necessary.

1. _____

_____

2. _____

_____

3. _____

_____

4. _____

_____

5. _____

_____

6. _____

_____

7. _____

_____

8. _____

_____

EXERCISE 6

Check (✔) the sentence—(a) or (b)—closest in meaning to each statement.

1. While Mr. Meyer was brushing his teeth, someone entered the room.
   ____ a. Mr. Meyer finished brushing his teeth, before someone entered.
   ✓ b. Mr. Meyer was alone when he started brushing his teeth.

2. When he got Mrs. Meyer's call, Phil Fork left his office and drove to her house.
   ✓ a. Mrs. Meyer called before Phil Fork left his office.
   ____ b. Mrs. Meyer called after Phil Fork left his office.

3. As soon as he got into his car, he took out a cigarette and lit it.
   ____ a. He was smoking when he got into the car.
   ✓ b. He started to smoke after he got into his car.

4. While Fork was driving to the Meyers' house, he was listening to his favorite opera on the radio.
   ✓ a. He drove his car and listened to the radio at the same time.
   ____ b. He turned on the radio when he reached the Meyers' house.

5. When he got there, a number of police officers were searching the house for clues.
   ____ a. They started when he got there.
   ✓ b. They started before he got there.

6. As soon as Fork started to question Mrs. Meyer, she burst into tears.
   ____ a. She was crying when he started to question her.
   ✓ b. She started to cry when he began to question her.

7. Phil Fork carefully reviewed all his notes when he went home.
   ✓ a. He went home first.
   ____ b. He reviewed his notes first.

(handwritten notes in margins: "Resolute light → encender (pasado)"; "a llorar / Explotar laginos"; "lit it"; "burst")

EXERCISE 7

Work with a partner and write down five things you know about John Lennon.

Here is some more information about John Lennon's life. The wavy line (∿∿∿∿∿) indicates an action in progress. X indicates a completed action.

1. attend high school	2. attend high school
∿∿∿∿	∿∿∿∿
X	X
his mother dies	meet Paul McCartney
3. study at art school	4. perform in clubs in Liverpool
∿∿∿∿	∿∿∿∿
X	X
form the Beatles	sign his first recording contract
5. tour America	6. live in London
∿∿∿∿	∿∿∿∿
X	X
appear on the *Ed Sullivan Show*	fall in love with Yoko Ono
7. work for peace and write new songs	8. leave his apartment
∿∿∿∿∿∿ X	∿∿∿∿ X
die	one of his fans shoots him

Use this information to finish the short biography below. Fill in the blanks, using the simple past or the past progressive. The first one has been done for you as an example.

John Lennon was one of the most famous singer/songwriters of his time. He was born in Liverpool, England, in 1940, but his childhood was not very happy.

(1) ___His mother died___ while ___he was attending high school___. Life was diffcult for John after his mother's death, but after a time things got better.
(2) _He met Paul He_ while _he was attending High School_. Soon Paul introduced him to George Harrison, and they began to play in a band together. After John left high school, he became an art student. (3) While _He was studing_, _He formed the Beatle_. After forming the Beatles, John married his first wife, Cynthia, and they had a son, Julian. (4) _He was performing_ in clubs in liverpool when _He signed his first recording Contract_. John and the Beatles moved to London and became very famous. They traveled all over the world. (5) While _He was touring_, America. _He appeared on the_, a popular television show at the time. Show Sullivan. (6) _____ while _____. A couple of years later, the Beatles split up. John and Yoko got married and moved to the United States, where their son Sean was born. John (7) _was working for peace an writing new songs._ when _He Died_. On December 8, 1980, (8) _One of his fans shooted him_ while _He was leaving his apartment._

John Lennon died in 1980, but he still has lots of fans all over the world.

while ◡(ing)
when ◡(ed)

brackets ()

EXERCISE 8

Complete the sentences in the story below using the words in parentheses. Use the simple past or the past progressive. The first one has been done for you.

1. Wangari Maathai ____received____ (receive) the Nobel Peace Prize in 2004.
2. While Wangari *was growing up* (grow up) in Kenya, the land around her home *had* (have) plenty of trees and water.
3. While she *was studing* (study) biology in college in the United States and at the University of Nairobi, she *realized* (realize) the importance of plants and animals to the environment.
4. When she *returned* (return) home, she *found* (find) that large companies *were destroying* (destroy) the forests. Many of the trees and rivers were already gone.
5. When she *asked* (ask) poor women from her village about their problems, they *told* (tell) her how they walked many miles every day to get firewood and water.
6. So she *worked* (work) with these women to plant trees and *created* (create) the Green Belt Movement in 1977. In thirty years, they planted 30 million trees.
7. Before she *started* (start) to work with the women, they *didn't feel* (not + feel) they had any power to change their lives.
8. Some people *attacked* (attack) her, and she was injured while she *was planting* (plant) trees in the Karura Public Forest in Nairobi, Kenya.
9. The Kenyan Government *arrested* (arrest) her many times.
10. When Wangari *received* (receive) the Nobel Peace Prize in 2004, she *made* (make) a speech. She said that wars start because of unequal distribution of resources: "A healthy environment is the path to peace."

Use Your English

Nan Silviera has just written her first book:
   As you can see below, the author's life story on the back of the book is not complete. Work with a partner to finish writing it.

■ **STEP 1**   Student A: Turn to page 103. Student B: Turn to page A-16.

■ **STEP 2**   You both have information about Nan's life, but some of the information is missing. Do not show your pages to each other, but ask each other questions to get information about the parts marked "?".

■ **STEP 3**   Write down the information your partner gives you so that when you finish, you will have the complete story.

■ **STEP 4**   Use the information from your chart to write the story of Nan's life. You can use the biography on the back of her book to begin writing.

■ **STEP 5**   When you finish writing, check your work to see if you have used time clauses and the past progressive and simple past tenses appropriately.

About the author
Nan Silveira graduated from Arizona State University. In 1991 she sailed solo across the Pacific. After that she...

JOURNEYS
By
Nan Silviera

ACTIVITY **2** speaking/listening/writing

In this activity, you will be gathering information about your classmates' lives by asking what they were doing at the times shown below. In the last box on the chart, add a time of your own choice (for example, on your last birthday, last New Year's Eve, etc.). Do not write information about yourself.

■ **STEP 1** Think about the different students in your class. Can you guess what they were doing at these times? In the box marked *Guesses*, write what **you** think different people were doing at each time.

■ **STEP 2** Go around the room and talk to as many people as possible to find out what they were really doing.

■ **STEP 3** Write this information in the box marked *Facts*.

NOTE: Copy the chart into your notebook if you need more space to write. If you don't want to give information about a certain time, you can say, "I'm sorry but I'd rather not talk about that time." If you can't remember, you can invent something.

TIMES	GUESSES	FACTS
at 8:30 P.M last Sunday		
in May 1993		
five years ago		
ten years ago today		
????? (you choose a time)		

■ **STEP 4** When you finish, review the information you collected. Choose the most interesting or surprising facts and make a short report (oral or written). Report on the facts, not on your original guesses. For example:

I asked my classmates about certain times in their lives. For example, at 8:30 P.M. yesterday, Sun Wu was working on her homework, and Tran was at home watching TV.

ACTIVITY 3 speaking/writing

■ **STEP 1** Take a large sheet of paper and make a time line for your own life like the one used on page 103. Bring your time line to class and describe the story of your life to your classmates.

■ **STEP 2** Exchange your time line with a partner. Use his or her time line to write the story of your partner's life. How many differences and similarities can you find between your partner's life history and yours?

ACTIVITY 4 speaking/listening/writing

On December 26, 2004, a huge tidal wave—called a tsunami—hit many countries of Southeast Asia including Indonesia, Thailand, Sri Lanka, and India. The giant wave—up to100 feet high in some places—was caused by an earthquake under the Indian Ocean off the coast of Sumatra. The tsunami killed about 275,000 people and was one of the worst natural disasters in modern history. The tsunami is sometimes called the Boxing Day Tsunami because it took place on December 26, which is a holiday called Boxing Day in many countries. Do you remember what you were doing when you heard about the Boxing Day Tsunami?

■ **STEP 1** With a partner, interview one or two people about what they were doing when they heard the news of the Boxing Day or Asian Tsunami. If possible, record your interviews. Before the interview, get together with your partner to make a list of possible questions. You can use the questions below or make other questions of your own, if you prefer.

■ **STEP 2** Share the results of your interviews with the class.

■ **STEP 3** Listen to your recording and write down any sentences with the simple past or the past progressive. Underline any time clauses in these sentences.

- What were you doing when you heard the news of the Boxing Day Tsunami?
- Where were you living at that time?
- Who were you with?
- What did you do after you heard about it?
- How did you feel?
- Add your own questions.

ACTIVITY 5 listening

For this activity, you will hear three conversations with people being interviewed about what they were doing when they heard about the Boxing Day Asian Tsunami.

CD Tracks
9,10,11

■ **STEP 1** Listen to the audio and take notes in the chart below.

CONVERSATION	PLACE	WHAT WAS THIS PERSON DOING?	WHAT DID THIS PERSON DO AFTER THAT?
Speaker 1	at home in Florida		
Speaker 2			
Speaker 3			

■ **STEP 2** Listen to the audio again and write down any examples of the past progressive or simple past.

ACTIVITY 6 research on the web

On the Web: Think of a famous person you want to know more about. Go to the Internet and use a search engine such as Google® or Yahoo® to find information about his or her life. Type the name of the person and *biography*. Draw a brief time line of the main events in his or her life. Show the time line to your classmates and explain the sequence of events.

ACTIVITY 7 reflection

Think of three key events in your life. What happened? Why were they important? Make sentences using time clauses to describe these events. Try to use the different time clauses you learned in this unit.

Activity 1 (from p.99)
Student A

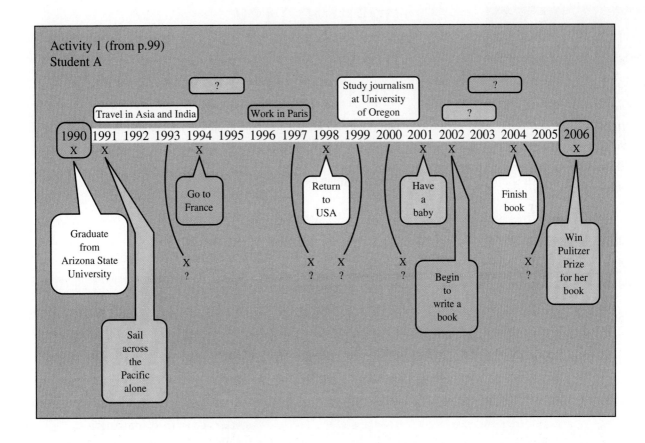

SIMILARITIES AND DIFFERENCES
Comparatives, Superlatives, *As . . . As, Not As . . . As*

- Use comparatives and superlatives to express differences

- Understand the meaning of *as . . . as* and *not as . . . as*

- Form sentences with *as . . . as* and *not as . . . as*

- Use *as . . . as* and *not as . . . as* to make tactful comparisons

OPENING TASK
Friends

■ STEP 1

Can you guess the names of the people in the picture? Work by yourself or with a partner. Use the information in the chart and the list of clues to identify each person. Write their names in the correct position on the picture.

The Left  The Right

NAME	AGE	OCCUPATION	HAIR	HEIGHT
LINDA	75	doctor	short, white	5'9 1/2"
BOB	21	student	medium-length, brown	5'9 1/2"
SUSAN	25	student	long, blond	5'1"
FRANK	43	artist	short, gray	6'4"
CARLA	28	singer	medium-length, black	5'5"
GEORGE	44	writer	bald	5'10"
DIANA	58	engineer	medium-length, brown	5'10"

Clues

1. The oldest person is next to the youngest person.
2. The tallest woman is in front of someone thirty years younger than she is.
3. The shortest person is in front of someone with white hair.
4. The tallest man is next to the tallest woman.
5. The 28-year-old is in front of the youngest person.
6. The man with short wavy hair is not quite as tall as the person next to him on the right.
7. The man on the right of the youngest person is behind the tallest person.
8. The youngest person is as tall as the person next to him on the left.

When you finish, check your answers with the rest of the class to see if you all agree. You can find the solution to the Opening Task on page A-17.

STEP 2

Work in pairs. Describe one person in the picture by comparing him or her with the other people. Your partner will guess which person you are describing.

Example: *She's taller than Susan, but has shorter hair than Diana. (Answer: Linda)*

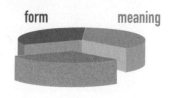

FOCUS 1 — Expressing Difference: Comparatives and Superlatives

EXAMPLES	EXPLANATIONS
(a) Susan is **the shortest**, and Frank is **the tallest**.	*The tallest* and *the shortest* are superlatives. Superlatives show extremes of difference among people or things. They show which has the greatest amount of a certain quality in a group of people or things.

Susan   Frank

EXAMPLES	EXPLANATIONS
(b) George is taller than Linda. (c) Carla is shorter than George.	*Taller than* and *shorter than* are comparatives. Comparatives show differences among people or things, but they do not show extremes of difference.

Carla Linda George

Comparatives and superlatives can be used with all parts of speech:

	Comparative	Superlative	
young	younger **than**	**the** young**est**	• adjectives with one syllable
easy	easi**er than**	the easi**est**	• adjectives with one syllable + -*y*
difficult	**more/less** difficult **than**	**the most/the least** difficult	• adjectives with two or more syllables
carefully	**more/less** carefully **than**	**the most/the least** carefully	• adverbs
weigh	weigh **more/less than**	weigh **the most/the least**	• verbs
money	**more/less** money **than**	**the most/the least** money	• nouns

(d) George sings **better (worse)** than I do.

(e) Carla is the **best (worst)** singer in the family.

Some comparative and superlative forms are irregular. Examples (d) and (e) use irregular comparative and superlative forms of *good* and *bad*.

EXERCISE 1

First fill in the blanks with a word or word ending, and then use the information from the Opening Task to decide if the statements are true (T) or false (F).

1. The oldest woman is taller __than__ the oldest man.   T (F)
2. George is tall __er__ than the person beside him.   (T) F
3. Diana is young __er__ __than__ the man beside her on the right.   T (F)
4. George is tall __er__ __than__ Frank.   T (F)
5. The singer is several years older __than__ the person behind her.   (T) (F)
6. The doctor is __the__ old __est__.   (T) F
7. Bob is old __er__ __than__ the person in front of him.   T (F)
8. The young __est__ woman is in front of __the__ old __est__ woman.   (T) F
9. Frank is __the__ tall __est__ man, but he isn't __the__ old __est__.   (T) F
10. __the__ old __est__ man is short __er__ __than__ the young __est__ woman.   (T) F

Now write three statements about the people in the box found in the Opening Task. They can be True (T) or False (F). Show them to your partner. Your partner will decide if they are true or false.

Example: *The doctor is taller than Carla.* (False)

EXERCISE 2

Work with a partner. Read the information at right about working hours and vacation times. Ask your partner questions about each person, using the comparative and the superlative. Or, write down the questions and share them with a partner or the class.

NAME	WORKING HOURS	VACATION TIME
LINDA	8 A.M.–5 P.M.	4 weeks
BOB	9 A.M.–4 P.M.	12 weeks
SUSAN	9 A.M.–4 P.M.	12 weeks
FRANK	6 A.M.–1 P.M.	none
CARLA	9 P.M.–2 A.M.	6 weeks
GEORGE	7 A.M.–3 P.M.	3 weeks
DIANA	9 A.M.–5 P.M.	2 weeks

Examples:
    A: *Who starts work the earliest?*
    B: *Frank does.*
    A: *Who finishes work later, Susan or Linda?*
    B: *Linda.*

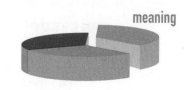

FOCUS 2 Similarity and Difference: *As . . . As* and *Not As . . . As*

EXAMPLES	EXPLANATIONS
Linda is about 5'9". Bob is about 5'9". (a) Linda is **as tall as** Bob. OR Bob is **as tall as** Linda. 	To show similarity among people or things, you can use *as . . . as*.
(b) George is **exactly as tall as** Diana. OR Diana is **exactly as tall as** George. 	To show that people or things are the same, you can add *exactly*.
George is 5'10". Bob is 5'9 1/2". (c) Bob is $\begin{cases} \text{almost} \\ \text{not quite} \\ \text{nearly} \\ \text{practically} \\ \text{just about} \end{cases}$ as tall as George 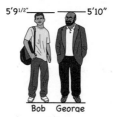	To show that people or things are very similar, add: *almost, not quite, nearly, practically*, or *just about*.
George is 5'10". Bob is 5'9 1/2". (d) Bob is **not as tall as** George.	To show differences among people or things, you can use *not as . . . as*.
Susan is 5'1". Diana is 5'10". (e) Susan is $\begin{cases} \text{nowhere near} \\ \text{not nearly} \\ \text{not anywhere near} \end{cases}$ as tall as Diana. 	To show a great amount of difference, add: *nowhere near, not nearly*, or *not anywhere near*. *Nowhere near* and *not anywhere near* are only used in very informal conversation with friends.

EXERCISE 3

Get together with another student. Think of all the ways that you are similar and all the ways that you are different. You have five minutes to make as many sentences as you can, using *as . . . as* and *not as . . . as* to show these differences and similarities. Share your sentences with the rest of the class.

Example: *Fernando isn't quite as tall as I am.*

EXERCISE 4

Use the information in the Opening Task to write complete sentences about the following people. You can use a comparative, a superlative, *as . . . as,* or *not as . . . as* in each sentence. Show the amount of difference or similarity as necessary.

1. Linda/Bob/height
   <u>Linda is as tall as Bob.</u>

2. Susan/Frank/height
   <u>Susan is not as tall as Frank.</u>

3. Linda/Diana/height
   <u>Diana is almost as tall as Diana.</u>

4. Linda/Carla/height
   <u>Carla is not as tall as Linda.</u>

5. George/Susan/height and age
   <u>Susan is not as tall as old than george.</u>

6. Bob/George/height
   <u>Bob is just about as tall as George.</u>

7. Frank/George/age
   <u>Frank is almost as young as george.</u>

8. Diana/Linda/age
   <u>Linda is oldher than Diana.</u>

9. Frank/height
   <u>Frank is the tallerst</u>

10. Linda/age
    <u>Linda is the Odenst.</u>

11. George/Diana/height
    <u>George is as tall as Diana</u>

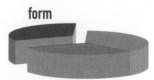

FOCUS 3   Using *As . . . As* and *Not As . . . As*

EXAMPLES	EXPLANATIONS
(a) Susan is **not as tall as** Carla. (b) Frank does not work **as quickly as** George. (c) Linda does not have **as much money as** Diana. (d) Diana does not have **as many friends as** Carla. (e) George **works as** much **as** Linda.	*As . . . as* and *not as . . . as* can be used with all parts of speech: • adjectives • adverbs • noncount nouns • count nouns • verbs
(f) Susan works as hard as **Carla works.** (g) Carla is not as tall as **Linda is.** (h) Susan works as hard as **Carla does.** (i) Susan works as hard as **Carla.** (j) Carla is not as tall as **her younger sister.** (k) Susan works as hard as **I/you/he/she/we/they.**	In sentences using *as . . . as* or *not as . . . as*, the second *as* can be followed by: • clauses • reduced clauses • noun phrases • subject pronouns
(l) Susan works as hard as he **works.** OR (m) Susan works as hard as he **does.**	In sentences where the verb is repeated after the second *as*, you can use a form of *do* instead.
(n) Susan works **as hard as he.** OR (o) Susan works **as hard as him.**	The same verb does not need to be repeated a second time. Using the subject pronoun (*he, she, I, we, you, they*) here is very formal. The object pronoun (*him, her, me, us, you, them*) is very common in conversation and informal writing.

(p) Susan's hair is not as short as **mine.**
 	
(q) Susan's hair is as long
    as **mine.**
 	
Susan's   My
Hair   Hair
 	
(r) Susan's hair is as long as me.
    Susan's
    Hair   Me
	Remember to use a possessive pronoun where necessary.
	In examples (q) and (r), both sentences are correct, but there is a big difference in meaning!

EXERCISE 5

Correct the mistakes in the following sentences.

Example: *Miriam is more serious ~~as~~ than her sister, Hester.*

1. All her life, Hester has been lucky (luckier) than her sister, Miriam. ✓

2. Hester is not (as) intelligent as Miriam, but she was always more successful than Miriam in school. ✓

3. For example, Hester's grades were always better than Miriam.'s grade ✓

4. Both sisters are pretty, but many people believe that Miriam is prettier that (than) her sister.

5. However, Miriam does not have as many boyfriends than (as) her sister does. ✓

6. They both have excellent jobs, but Miriam thinks her job isn't as interesting as her sister.'s (job).

7. They both travel as part of their work, but Hester goes to more exciting places than Miriam is (does).

8. In spite of these differences, Miriam thinks that she is happier that (than) her sister is. ✓

9. However, Hester thinks that good luck is (more) important than good looks and intelligence. ✓

What do **you** think is the most important: good luck, good looks, or intelligence? Why do you think so? Share your ideas with your classmates.

Work in a group to create a problem like the one in the Opening Task. First use the picture and blank chart below to record your information and then write the clues. Each clue must contain at least one of the following: a comparative, a superlative, *as . . . as,* or *not as . . . as.* Finally, exchange your problem with that from another group and see if you can solve each other's problems.

front.

left. *Right*

Behind.

NAME	AGE	HEIGHT	OCCUPATION	WORKING HOURS
Martine	46.	1.66	Officer	8 hours
Luisa	29.	1.60.	House wife.	full time.
Patricia	38.	1.69	Desperate Housewife.	Full Time.
Fernanda	28.	1.64.	Laywer	10 hours.
Jean Marie	39.	1.65.	Resource (Epidemiologist)	12 to 14 hours.

Clues

- the laywer is in front of the Epidemiologist
- the Tallest woman is next to the smaller woman person
- the Olderst is in front of the Tallest woman.
- the Epidemiologist is next to the Laywer. woman.
- the person who works 8 hours per day is in front of the Desperate housewife.

FOCUS 4 | Making Tactful Comparisons with As . . . As and Not As . . . As

use

Sometimes it is important to be tactful (more polite and less direct) when you are making comparisons. The adjective you choose can show how tactful your comparison is.

EXAMPLES	EXPLANATIONS
Some adjectives commonly used in making comparisons: Express "MORE":	Express "LESS":	When you use *as . . . as*, it is more common or usual to use an adjective that expresses "more." When you use an adjective that expresses "less," you draw special attention to it because it is an unusual use.

Express "MORE":	Express "LESS":
tall	*short*
old	*young*
large	*small*
fast	*slow*

(a) Linda is **as tall as** Bob.	In (a), the use of *tall* is usual. It does not make us think about **how** tall or **how** short Bob and Linda are, but only that they are the same height.
(b) Linda is **as short as** Bob.	In (b), the use of *short* is unusual. It makes us think that both Bob and Linda are very short.
(c) Patricia is **as old as** Virginia.	In (c), the use of *old* is usual. It shows only that they are the same age.
(d) Patricia is **as young as** Virginia.	In (d), the use of *young* is unusual. It therefore puts special emphasis on *young*.
(e) Bob is **not as tall as** Frank. (f) Frank is **not as short as** Bob. Bob Frank	Both (e) and (f) show that Frank is taller than Bob. However, the use of *short* in (f) is unusual, so it draws special attention to the fact that Bob is short. It is more tactful and more polite to choose (e).
(g) Otis is **not quite as smart as** Rocky. (h) His latest book is **not quite as good as** his earlier ones.	When you want to be really polite and tactful, you can use *not quite as . . . as*.

EXERCISE 7

You are the manager of a large company. A smaller company wants to do business with you but there are several problems to discuss. They will have to improve their overall performance before you are willing to do business with them.

Use the adjectives in parentheses with *not as . . . as*. Add *not quite* if you want to be even more tactful. The first one has been done for you.

1. Your company is smaller than ours. (large)

   <u>Your company is not as large as ours.</u>

2. Your factories are more old-fashioned than ours. (modern)

   _____

3. Your workers are lazier than ours. (energetic)

   _____

4. Your products are less popular than ours. (well known)

   _____

5. Your advertising is less successful than ours. (effective)

   _____

6. Your designs are more conservative than ours. (up-to-date)

   _____

7. Your production is slower than ours. (fast)

   _____

8. The quality of your product line is lower than ours. (high)

   _____

9. Your factories are dirtier than ours. (clean)

   _____

10. Your factories are more dangerous than ours. (safe)

    _____

Omar is president of the International Students' Association at an American college. He wants to write an article for the college newspaper about international students' reactions to life in America. He made a survey of the international students. Help him to write the answers in a more tactful and polite way.

1. Children in America watch more TV.

   Children in my country don't watch as much TV as they do in America.

2. People have dinner very early in America.

   _____

3. People eat more fast food in America.

   _____

4. Food is cheaper in America.

   _____

5. Americans work longer hours than people in my country.

   _____

6. People change jobs more easily in America.

   _____

7. Cities are cleaner in America.

   _____

8. People drive longer distances in America than in my country.

   _____

Do you agree or disagree with these comments? Do you have any comments of your own that Omar could include in his article? Add them here:

_____

_____

_____

_____

Use Your English

ACTIVITY 1 speaking/writing

■ **STEP 1** Work in groups. Imagine that someone from your country (or a country that you know well) is going to stay with a family in America. Discuss and make notes about the differences in culture and customs they may find surprising. Include information about the best places in town for international students to meet new people and to practice English.

■ **STEP 2** Divide your group into small groups of two or three people. One small group will write a brief guide for the American host family. The other pair will write a guide for the visiting student. Be tactful where necessary!

ACTIVITY 2 writing

You are staying with an American family for the summer. Write a letter to your own family describing some of the differences you have experienced between life in America and life in your country. Before you start, make a list of interesting, surprising, or reassuring topics.

ACTIVITY 3 speaking/listening

There are many common idioms in English that use the construction *as . . . as*. Some common idioms are:
- as strong as an ox
- as stubborn as a rule
- as quiet as a mouse

Interview several speakers of English and ask them to tell you as many idioms as they can remember. Write the idioms in your notebook and also write an example of when they might use each idiom. Choose one of these new idioms to explain to your classmates.

ACTIVITY 4 speaking/listening

The purpose of this activity is to think of as many differences as possible between two objects. Your teacher will tell you what you are to compare. Form teams. You have five minutes with your team to make a list of as many differences as possible. After five minutes, the teams take turns sharing their differences. The team with the most differences scores a point. Your teacher will then give you the next two objects to compare. The team with the most points is the winner.

■ **STEP 1**   To score a point, your comparison must be meaningful **and** accurate.

■ **STEP 2**   You cannot repeat a comparison that another team has already given. However, you **can** express the same idea, using different words. For example:

> **Team A says:** *A Harley Davidson motorcycle is more expensive than some cars.*
>
> **Team B can say:** *Some cars aren't as expensive as a Harley Davidson.*
>
> **Team C can say:** *Some cars are cheaper than a Harley Davidson . . .*
>
> and so on.

If possible, try to record your team as you play this game. Afterwards listen to the recording and see how many comparative, superlative, and (*not*) *as . . . as* forms you used.

ACTIVITY 5 speaking/listening

■ **STEP 1**   Choose one set of objects that you compared in Activity 4. Ask three different people outside of class to compare these two objects and record their replies. Listen to the recording. Did they make more comparisons than you did? Or did you make more comparisons than them? Compare your findings with classmates.

■ **STEP 2**   Listen to your recording again and write down any sentences with examples of comparative, superlative, and (*not*) *as . . . as* forms.

ACTIVITY 6 listening/speaking

CD Track 12

■ **STEP 1**

Before you listen to the audio for this activity, get together with a partner. Make a list of all the differences you can think of between working for a small company and working for a large company. Write them on the left side of a chart in your notebook.

What are the differences between working for a small company and a large company?

DIFFERENCES: _____ (partner) and I	DIFFERENCES: TERRY AND ROBIN
A small company is friendlier than a large company.	

■ **STEP 2**

Listen to the audio. You will hear two people, Terry and Robin, compare working for a small company and working for a large company. Add the differences they describe to the right side of the chart. How many differences did you and your partner find? How many did Terry and Robin find?

■ **STEP 3**

Now listen to the audio again, and write down any sentences with comparative, superlative, or *(not) as . . . as* forms in them.

ACTIVITY 7 speaking

■ **STEP 1**

Think of two jobs that you had in the past. Tell your partner about them. Say which one you liked better and why. Report to the class about your partner's jobs.

■ **STEP 2**

Make a list of adjectives or adverbs you used in your report. Group the words according to those that use *-er* or *-est* , those that use "more" or "most," and other words that show similarity or difference. Can you find a pattern?

ACTIVITY 8 speaking/listening

We sometimes honor people with special awards for achievements in different fields. For example, the film industry presents Oscars every year for "the best picture," "the best director," and so on. This year, your school will give several special awards for different achievements. You and your classmates are on the committee that will decide who should get these awards.

■ **STEP 1**   In small groups, make a list of awards you would like to give. For example, you can give awards for "the best dressed student," "the most talkative student," "the most creative dancer," "the student who is the most likely to become president of his or her country," and so on. Decide on who should receive these awards. You can also give awards to other people on campus or to places that you like in the community, for example, "the teacher who gives the most homework," "the best hamburger," "the quietest place to study," "the best place to meet other students."

■ **STEP 2**   Hold a class awards "ceremony" to announce the winners and present the awards.

ACTIVITY 9 research on the web

InfoTrac® College Edition: Go to *InfoTrac* to read facts about two countries: for example, Russia and the United States. Type: "Compare facts: Russia and the United States" Write five sentences comparing these two countries and tell the class. What explanations can you think of for the similarities and differences you found?

ACTIVITY 10 reflection

What similarities or differences are there between English and your first language (or another language you know well)? Which one is easier or more difficult and why? Make a list of differences and similarities and present your list to the class.

MEASURE WORDS AND QUANTIFIERS

UNIT GOALS

- Understand special measure words used with foods

- Use measure words with count and noncount nouns

- Know how to use common quantifiers

OPENING TASK

Getting Ready for a Potluck Dinner

■ STEP 1

Jim has been invited to a potluck dinner—a meal where each guest brings a dish. The hostess asked him to bring cookies and a salad for six people. Look at the picture of Jim's kitchen. Can you name the different foods? How much does he have of each food?

STEP 2

Jim wants to make everything himself. He already has these ingredients in his kitchen.

INGREDIENTS	
mustard	chocolate chips
sugar	tomatoes
salt	flour
lettuce	olive oil
hard-boiled eggs	butter
cheese	eggs
vinegar	garlic

Help Jim decide which ingredients he can use in each dish. Write each ingredient in the box below.

SALAD	SALAD DRESSING	CHOCOLATE CHIP COOKIES

STEP 3

How much of each ingredient do you think Jim should use? Write an amount beside each ingredient. Remember, there will be six people at the party.

STEP 4

Are there any **other** ingredients you would include? Add them to the boxes above, with suggested amounts.

FOCUS 1   Measure Words with Food

CONTAINERS

Some measure words are **containers** that we can find in a store.

a bottle of (soy sauce, ketchup)

a jar of (peanut butter, mustard)

a box of (cereal, crackers)

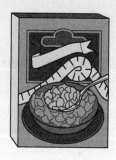

a bag of (potato chips, flour)

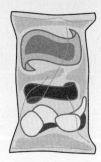

a carton of (milk, eggs)

a can of (tuna fish, soup)

PORTIONS

Some measure words are **portions**. They describe food items as they are commonly served.

a slice of (bread, cheese)

a scoop of ice cream

a piece of (cake, candy)

a cube of sugar

a strip of bacon

MEASUREMENTS

In North America, these **measurements** are common in recipes:

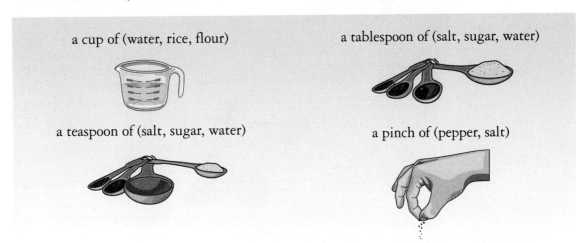

a cup of (water, rice, flour)

a tablespoon of (salt, sugar, water)

a teaspoon of (salt, sugar, water)

a pinch of (pepper, salt)

SHAPES AND TYPICAL STATES

Some measure words talk about the **shape** or **appearance** of the food item.

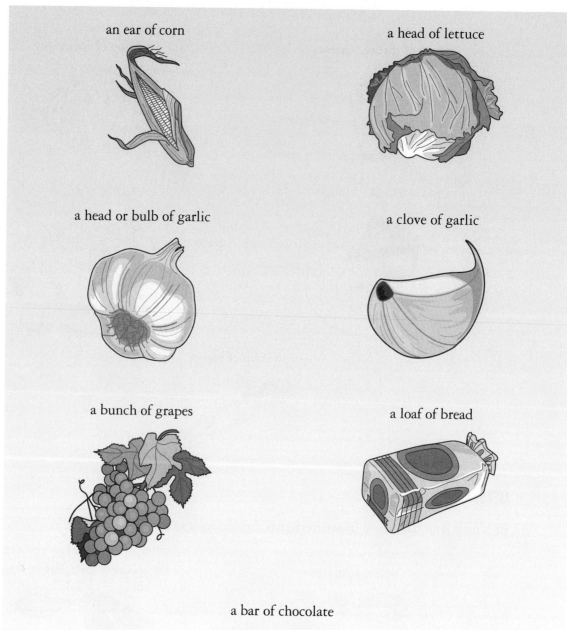

an ear of corn

a head of lettuce

a head or bulb of garlic

a clove of garlic

a bunch of grapes

a loaf of bread

a bar of chocolate

EXERCISE 1

Turn back to the Opening Task on page 121. Look at the ingredients and the amounts. Did you use the right measure words? Make any necessary corrections.

EXERCISE 2

Turn back to the Opening Task and look carefully at the ingredients. Some of these are count nouns (tomatoes) and some are noncount nouns (flour). Write C beside each count noun and NC beside each noncount noun.*

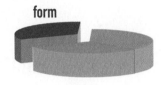

form

FOCUS 2	Measure Words with Count and Noncount Nouns

Measure words express specific quantities. They also allow us to make noncount nouns countable.

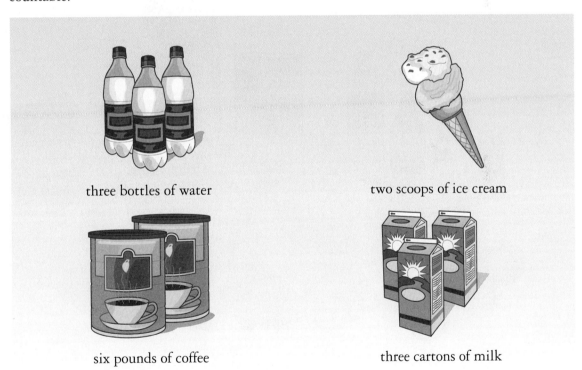

three bottles of water

two scoops of ice cream

six pounds of coffee

three cartons of milk

*For more information on count and noncount nouns, see *Grammar Dimensions* Book 1, Unit 4.

Most measure expressions follow this pattern.*

A/An/One Two Three	+	Measure Word (Singular/Plural)	+	of	+	Noun (Noncount/Plural)
a		cup		of		milk
a		pound		of		apples
two		cups		of		milk
two		pounds		of		apples

* Exception: specific numbers (including *dozen*):
         a dozen eggs NOT a dozen of eggs
         ten strawberries NOT ten of strawberries

▮ EXERCISE 3

These are the recipes that Jim finally used. Complete the missing parts. (The picture may help you.)

Jim's Super Salad

1 large (a) ———————————— of red lettuce

1 medium-sized (b) ———————————— of romaine lettuce

1 large cucumber, cut into (c) ————————————

6 tomatoes, cut into quarters

$^1/_2$ (d) ———————————— of Swiss cheese, cut into small strips

1 (e) ———————————— cooked chicken, shredded into small pieces

2 hard-boiled eggs, shelled and cut into quarters

1. Line a large salad bowl with red lettuce leaves.
2. Tear the romaine lettuce leaves into medium-sized pieces.
3. Place in the bowl in layers: slices of cucumber and tomato, cheese, lettuce, and chicken.
4. Add olives and eggs. Cover and refrigerate for one hour. Toss with Jim's Super Salad Dressing just before serving.

Jim's Super Salad Dressing

1 (a) ———————————— Dijon mustard $^1/_2$ (d) ———————————— salt

4 (b) ———————————— red wine vinegar $^1/_2$ (e) ———————————— pepper

1 (c) ———————————— sugar $^1/_2$ (f) ———————————— olive oil

1. Put the mustard into a bowl. Whisk in vinegar, sugar, salt, and pepper.
2. Slowly add the oil while continuing to whisk the mixture.

Jim's Granny's Old Time Chocolate Chip Cookies

$^1/_2$ (a) _____ butter

1 (b) _____ brown sugar

$^3/_4$ (c) _____
granulated sugar

2 eggs

2 (d) _____ flour

1 (e) _____ baking soda

1 (f) _____ vanilla extract

1 (g) _____ salt

1 $^1/_2$ (h) _____ chocolate chips

1. Preheat the oven to 350°F. Grease a cookie sheet.
2. Cream the butter and both the sugars together until light and fluffy. Add the eggs and vanilla and mix well.
3. Sift the flour, baking soda, and salt. Mix thoroughly.
4. Add the chocolate chips.
5. Form into cookies. Place on a cookie sheet and put on the middle rack of the oven for 8–10 minutes.
6. Cool for 5 minutes.
7. Enjoy! (This recipe makes about 40 cookies.)

Turn back to the Opening Task on page 121 and look at the ingredients (and the amounts) you suggested for these dishes. How many differences can you find between your suggestions and Jim's recipes? Whose recipe do you think will taste better?

EXERCISE 4

Last week Matthew ate a delicious spaghetti sauce at his friend Nancy's house. He enjoyed it so much that Nancy lent him the recipe so that he could make a copy of it. However, Nancy has obviously used this recipe many times and it is quite difficult to read. Can you help Matthew figure out the recipe? Fill in the missing words below.

> **Spaghetti Sauce**
>
> (from Nancy's kitchen)
>
> First, cut 3 _____ of bacon into small pieces and cook over a very low heat.
> Stir in $^1/_2$ a _____ of ground meat along with 4 _____ of garlic and 2
> _____ of onion, very finely chopped. Add 1 _____ of salt, a
> _____ of cayenne pepper, and 2 _____ of dried herbs. Mix in two
> 8-ounce _____ of tomato sauce. Cook on low heat for about 30 minutes.
> Serve over fresh pasta.

If you were making this recipe yourself, would you change or add anything? Share any changes or additions with your classmates. Try to be as precise as possible.

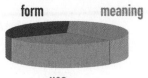
form   meaning

use

AMOUNT	EXAMPLES	EXPLANATIONS
all	(a) **All** of the dishes at the potluck were delicious. (b) He spends **all** of his money on wine.	Some quantifiers (words that talk about quantity/number or amount) can be used with **both count and noncount** nouns. Use *all* to mean *everything* or *everyone*.
most	(c) **Most** of the people in North America take vacations in the summer. (d) **Most** people in my town work in tourism.	Most means *almost everyone* or *almost everything*. Use *most of* when there is an article before the noun. Use *most* when there is no article.
many/much	(e) We heard that *many* people were coming. (f) We don't have *much* time. (g) A: Were *many* people hurt? (h) B: No, not *many*.	*Many* is used only with count nouns to talk about a large number. Use *much* with noncount nouns to talk about a large amount. *Many* and *much* are usually used in questions or negative statements.
a lot of *lots of* *a great deal of*	(i) We make *a lot of* trips back and forth over the mountains. (j) I heard that there was *lots of* new snow. (k) *A great deal of* current information is available on the Internet.	Use *a lot of* or *lots of* with very large numbers or amounts, and with either count or noncount nouns. *Lots of* is used in informal situations. Use *a great deal of* in formal situations, and only with noncount nouns. It means the same as *a lot of* or *lots*.
some	(l) We needed *some* milk for the recipe. (m) We were glad that we had put *some* new snow tires on our car.	*Some* is a smaller amount or quantity than *a lot of/lots of*. *Some* is used with both count and noncount nouns. *Continued on next page*

Continued from previous page

AMOUNT	EXAMPLES	EXPLANATIONS
several	(n) We couldn't travel on *several* days last winter because the mountain passes were closed.	*Several* is used only with count nouns. *Several* means more than a small number.
a few / a little	(o) In a *few* days, we'll be ready to go.	*A few* means more than two, but not many more.
	(p) There was *a little* snow on the mountains.	*A few* and *a little* have similar meanings. *A little* is used only with noncount nouns and *a few* is used only with count nouns.
	(q) Let's buy *a little* food and *a few* cans of soda.	
few/little	(r) We have *few* friends and *little* money.	*Few* and *little* refer to the same amounts or numbers as *a few* and *a little*; however, they have a negative meaning. They mean *almost none*.
	(s) *Few* people know that she has *little* time left.	*Few* is used only with count nouns, *little* only with noncount nouns.
a couple (of)	(t) I'd like to get *a couple of* blankets to keep in the car.	*A couple of* means two, but it is sometimes used informally to mean two or more.
	(u) Let's ask *a couple (of)* people to come with us.	*A couple of* is used only with count nouns. In informal English, *of* is sometimes omitted.
none/no	(v) *None of* the people went to the meeting.	*None* means *not any*, and is used with count nouns.
	(w) We heard that there was *no* new snow.	*No* has the same meaning, and is used with noncount nouns.

▌EXERCISE 5

Choose the correct quantifier for each sentence.

1. There are _____ big supermarkets in my town.

   a. a lot   b. a little   c. much   d. several

2. We usually get _____ of rain in the summer.

   a. a little   b. some   c. most   d. a lot

3. There are _____ fast-food restaurants near my house.

   a. a couple of   b. most   c. a little   d. a great deal of

4. _____ people have the Internet at home.

   a. None   b. Little   c. Few   d. A lot of

5. _____ education at my university concerns the use of new technology.

   a. All of   b. None of   c. Many of   d. A great deal of

Find a partner and take turns asking each other questions about your native countries or countries you know about. Use the topics in (A) to ask general questions. In your answers to the questions, give specific examples to explain what you mean. You must use a quantifier (from Focus 3) in your answer. Column (B) gives you ideas for quantifiers you can use in your answers, but you may use others.

Example: Q: *Is clothing expensive in (Vietnam)?*

A: *No, not really. A lot of people go to the big cities to buy clothes. There are lots of factories in the cities, so you can usually find clothes that are pretty cheap.*

(A) Topic	(B) Quantifier
1. clothing	some lots of/a lot of
2. tourist attractions	a few a couple of
3. holidays	most some
4. climate	no/none a great deal of
5. fast-food restaurants	some several
6. technology	a few many
7. English speakers	most a lot of
8. entertainment	all much

Some of the sentences in the following letter have errors with nouns and with quantifiers. Find the errors and correct them. When you have finished, check your answers with another student.

Dear Nell,

I think I'm going to like my new job. So far it's interesting, and I hope that it stays that way! There are several of people who work in the same office with me. At the moment I share a desk with Jessica, who just started a couple week ago, but our office manager just ordered new furnitures so that soon we will each have a desk of our own. There are lot of people in the building who share desks and computers, so I feel pretty lucky to have my own to work on.

Every morning Martha, the staff assistant, brings us each a cup of coffee. She already knows that I like sugars in my coffee but no milks. Martha also brings the mails to us, and she likes to give us many advice about how to be efficient. Two times a day I get at least fifty letter which I have to respond to, so I do listen to Martha's advices. A few her ideas have really been useful!

Some days I can do most of my business on the computer. Other days I need a little more informations from my customers, so I need to talk to them on the telephone. Every day there are some problem that I cannot handle. If there are only couple of problems, my coworker helps, but on the days when there are lot of problems, we call in Anna, the office supervisor. Already there have been several time when even Anna couldn't handle the problems, and so she has had to call in her supervisor.

So you can see that I'm busy, and at this point, I'm not bored.

Talk to you soon—

Love,

Elliott

Use Your English

ACTIVITY 1 writing/speaking

This "recipe" was written by an English teacher:

"Recipe" for the Perfect Student

Ingredients:

1 cup of motivation	1 cup of imagination
1 cup of determination	1 $^1/_2$ cups of willingness to make a guess
$^1/_2$ cup of patience	1 cup of independence
$^1/_2$ cup of tolerance	1 $^1/_2$ cups of cooperation with others
1 cup of laughter	1 pinch of fun

Combine ingredients and stir gently to bring out the best flavor.

What do you think the teacher meant by this?

Get together with a partner and create a "recipe" of your own. Here are some ideas, but you probably have plenty of your own:

- Recipe for a long-lasting marriage
- Recipe for the perfect partner
- Recipe for the perfect teacher
- Recipe for the perfect house
- Recipe for the perfect mother/father

Share your recipes with the rest of the class.

ACTIVITY 2 writing

Write a paragraph describing your perfect birthday party (real or imaginary). Before writing, make notes on the people, food, music, and activities. When you have written your paragraph, exchange it with another student. Underline the quantifiers. Were they used correctly?

Example: *My ideal birthday party would have a lot of food, many friends . . .*

ACTIVITY 3 speaking

Your class is scheduled for a weekend trip to a nearby national park or state forest. Transportation is provided, and a few small overnight cabins are available. But you will need to decide what food to bring, and also what other things you will need. Here are some ideas: sleeping bags, cooking pots, eating utensils (plates, cups, silverware), firewood, sports equipment, depending on the season (fishing poles? swimsuits? skis?).

Work in groups and come up with a list. Be specific about the quantities. Compare lists to make sure you haven't forgotten anything!

ACTIVITY 4 speaking/listening/writing

■ **STEP 1**   Organize an international potluck. Everyone in the class should prepare and bring a dish, preferably from his or her country. After the meal, have each person describe his or her recipe. If possible, record the descriptions.

■ **STEP 2**   Listen to the recording and write down the recipes. Collect all the recipes for an international cookbook. Make copies and distribute them to the class.

ACTIVITY 5 listening

CD Track 13

■ **STEP 1**   Listen to the audio of a person describing a recipe for a traditional North American dish.
1. What dish is the speaker describing?
2. When is this dish usually eaten?
3. What are the important ingredients in the dish?

■ **STEP 2**   Listen to the audio again, and this time write down the ingredients and amounts.

Work with a partner to make sure that you understand what each ingredient is, and then take turns reading each ingredient and the amount aloud. If you decide to make this dish, it is important that your recipe is accurate!

For each ingredient with a measure word, write the kind of measure word:

- If it is a **container,** mark it C.
- If it is a **shape/typical state,** mark it S.
- If it is a **portion,** mark it P.
- If it is a **measurement,** mark it M.

1. Do you recognize the measurements?
2. Do you know what teaspoon/tablespoon/cup is?

ACTIVITY 6   research on the web

 On the Web: Go on the Internet using a search engine such as Google® or Yahoo® and find a recipe for one of these dishes: potato salad/cheesecake/apple pie/carrot soup. Make a list of the ingredients. Then compare your list with a partner. What differences in the ingredients did you find?

ACTIVITY 7   reflection

Make a list of food and drink you had today. Organize your list with the correct measure word for each item. Compare your list with a partner.

Example: *a teaspoon of sugar, a slice of bread*

DEGREE COMPLEMENTS
Too, *Enough*, and *Very*

UNIT GOALS

- Understand the meaning of *enough*, *not enough*, and *too*

- Form correct sentences with *enough*, *not enough*, and *too*

- Know how to use *too much*, *too many*, *too little*, and *too few*

- Understand the difference between *too* and *very*

OPENING TASK
Looking for Somewhere to Live

What's your ideal home?

■ STEP 1

Get together with a partner and try to guess what these housing abbreviations mean. Read the classified housing ads below to help you work out the answers.

apt   kit   BR   DR   lg   furn   kit   mo

driveway.
unfurnished.

For Rent

1 1200 SQ FT BASEMENT	2 EAST VILLAGE
2 BR APT	Renovated lg studio apt w/new wood flrs. High
$700	ceilings: sunny: lg windows:
Newly Painted. Walk to center. Furn/unfurn. No pets. Call owner before 9 P.M.	lg walk-in closet: mod kit
(718) 555-1320	**$650/mo** 555-0479
3 GREENWICH VILLAGE	4 GREENWICH ST.
Charming 1BR; new kit & bath. Very quiet building	3 BR Bright: Big closets: full bath: lge kit. Nice gdn.
$875/mo. 555-4345	**Call Tim** 555-8246 **$1250/mo.**

STEP 2

Read the classified ads about different types of housing rentals. Then match the ads with the descriptions of different home hunters. Explain which homes are NOT suitable for these people.

a. Maria is looking for an unfurnished house or apartment with lots of light and plenty of closet space. She cannot pay more than $900 a month.
Best home: _#2___

b. Sandra and Suzanne are looking for a two-bedroom apartment with at least 1000 square feet. They can pay $800 a month.
Best home: _#7.___

c. Tony and Carla have two children and a dog. They need a garden and a big kitchen. They can pay around $1200 a month. _#4._
Best home: _Greenwich St.___

d. Peter is looking for a sunny furnished studio apartment in good condition. He can pay $700 a month. _#2_
Best home: _#East Village___

STEP 3

Work with a partner and complete the sentences. Make similar sentences about the other people.

Maria likes apartment _____ because _____. She does not like apartment _____ because _____. She does not like apartment _____ because _____. She does not like apartment _____ because _____.

STEP 4

Look back at all the ads. Which place would you choose? Why? Which places would you definitely NOT choose? Why?

(Solution to the Opening Task on page A-16)

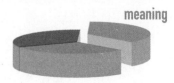

FOCUS 1 — Enough, Not Enough, Too

EXAMPLES	EXPLANATIONS
(a) There are **enough** closets. (b) This apartment is big **enough** for both of us.	*Enough* shows something is sufficient. You have as much as you need and you do not need any more. *Enough* usually shows that you are satisfied with the situation.
(c) There are **not enough** windows in this apartment. (I want more windows!) OR: There are**n't enough** windows in this apartment. (d) The bedroom is **not** big **enough**. (I want a bigger bedroom!) OR: The bedroom isn't **enough**.	*Not enough* shows that something is insufficient. In your opinion, there should be more. *Not enough* usually shows that you are not satisfied with the situation.
(e) The rent is **too** high. (It is more than I want to pay.) (f) The kitchen is **too** small. (I want a bigger one.) (g) That coffee is **too** hot. (I can't drink it.) (h) He speaks **too** fast. (I can't understand him.) (i) She's **too** young to drink. (She has to be 21 to drink alcohol in this state.)	*Too* shows that something is **more** than you want or need OR that it is **less** than you want or need. It depends on the meaning of the word that follows. *Too* usually shows that you are not satisfied with the situation.

EXERCISE 1

Look back at Step 2 of the Opening Task on page 137. Did you use *too, not enough,* or *enough*? If not, rewrite your reasons and see if you can use *too, enough,* or *not enough* in them.

Choose one of the families listed on page 137. In your opinion, what would each family say about these apartments? Where possible, use *too, enough,* and *not enough.*

1. Tiny but charming studio apartment. Large skylights. Limited storage space. $700.

Peter thinks the apartment has enough sky lights, but the storage space is not enough for him.

2. Gorgeous penthouse apartment. Fabulous views of Central Park. 3 bedrooms, 2 bathrooms. Dining room and roof garden. $1800.

the appartmeut has enought espace for him but is too expennue.

3. Bright two-bedroom apartment. Big closets. Next to fire station. $825.

the apartmeut has enought espace, but is too expennue.

EXERCISE 2

In this exercise, people are talking about problems that they are having, and their friends are responding by saying what they think caused these problems. For example:

I'm tired all the time.

You don't get enough sleep.

Read the list of problems and the list of causes below. What do you think caused the problems? Work with a partner and match the problems and their causes.

PROBLEMS		CAUSES
1. My feet really hurt.	__d__	a. You don't go to the dentist often enough.
2. I'm broke!	_____	b. Maybe you shouted too much at the ball game.
3. I failed my math test.	_____	c. You didn't add enough salt.
4. I've gained a lot of weight recently.	_____	d. Perhaps your shoes aren't big enough.
5. I never feel hungry at mealtimes.	_____	e. You spend too much money.
6. I can't sleep at night.	_____	f. Your stereo is too loud.
7. I have a sore throat.	_____	g. You don't get enough exercise.
8. This soup is tasteless.	_____	h. You eat too many snacks.
9. My neighbors are always angry with me.	_____	i. You drink too much coffee.
10. My teeth hurt.	_____	j. You didn't study enough.

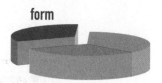

FOCUS 2   *Enough, Not Enough, Too*

EXAMPLES	EXPLANATIONS
(a) This house is **big enough.** That apartment is **not big enough.**	Place *enough* or *not enough*: • after adjectives
(b) Po speaks **clearly** enough. Tan does not speak **clearly enough.**	• after adverbs
(c) She **ate enough.** He **did not eat enough.**	• after verbs
(d) We have **enough money.** They **do not** have **enough money.**	• before nouns
(e) She is (not) **old enough to vote.**	Notice how *enough* can be used with: • an adjective + an infinitive
(f) They studied **hard enough to pass** the test, but they didn't study **hard enough to get** a good score.	• an adverb + an infinitive
(g) We (don't) **earn enough to pay** the rent.	• a verb + an infinitive
(h) I (don't) have **enough chocolate to make** a cake.	• a noun + infinitive
(i) She is **too young.**	Place *too* before adjectives and adverbs.
(j) They work **too slowly.**	
(k) This tea is **too hot to drink.**	*Too* + adjective or adverb is often followed by an infinitive.
(l) We worked **too late to go to** the party.	
(m) That book is **too difficult for me to understand.**	*Too* + adjective or adverb is often followed by *for* + noun/pronoun + infinitive.
(n) He walked **too fast for the children to keep up.**	

EXERCISE 3

Nazmi has some problems in his English classes. Rewrite the sentences using *too, enough,* or *not enough*. Compare your answers with a partner.

1. The teacher speaks too quietly.

   She doesn't _____ speak loudly enough _____.

2. Her writing is too small.

   Her writing is _____.

3. My seat is too far away from the board.

   My seat isn't _____.

4. The test time is too short and we never finish.

   There is _____.

5. I am too busy to finish all my homework.

   I don't _____.

6. Our grammar book isn't easy enough.

   Our grammar book is _____.

7. Our lessons aren't long enough.

   Our lessons are _____.

8. I have a lot of questions but I don't ask them.

   I don't _____.

9. I want to take the exam but I need to study more.

   I do _____.

10. I don't check my answers carefully enough.

    I check my answers _____.

Think of some other problems you have or know about. Describe the problem using *too,* or *not enough*. Take turns with a partner saying the same things in a different way.

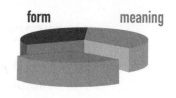

FOCUS 3 — *Too Much* and *Too Many*; *Too Little* and *Too Few*

EXAMPLES	EXPLANATIONS
(a) Walt has **too much money**.	Use *too much* with noncount nouns.
(b) There are **too many students** in this class.	Use *too many* with count nouns. *Too much* and *too many* show that there is more than you want or need. They show that you are not satisfied with the situation.
(c) There's **too little time** to finish this.	Use *too little* with noncount nouns.
(d) The class was canceled because **too few students** enrolled.	Use *too few* with count nouns. *Too little* and *too few* show that there is less than you want or need. They show that you are not satisfied with the situation.

EXERCISE 4

Read the following description of a wedding reception where everything went wrong. Underline all the words or phrases that show there was not enough of something. Where possible, replace these with *too little* or *too few* and change the verbs as necessary.

My sister's wedding was a disaster. First of all, she decided to get married very suddenly, so there <u>wasn't enough time to</u> ^(was too little time to) plan it properly. Nevertheless, about fifty of her friends came to the reception in her studio. Unfortunately, there wasn't enough room for everyone, so it was rather uncomfortable. She only had a few chairs, and our ninety-six-year-old grandmother had to sit on the floor. My father had ordered lots of champagne, but there weren't enough glasses, so some people didn't get very much to drink. In addition, we had several problems with the caterers. There wasn't enough cake for everyone, but there was too much soup! We also had problems with the entertainment. My sister loves Latin music, so she hired a salsa band; however, it was hard to move in such a small space, and my sister got upset when not enough people wanted to dance. I got into trouble too. I was the official photographer, but I didn't bring enough film with me, so now my sister is mad because she only has about ten wedding photographs—and all of them are pictures of people trying to find a place to sit down!

EXERCISE 5

You and your friends decided to give a big party. You made lots of plans, but unfortunately everything went wrong and the party was a total disaster. Get together with one or two other students and make a list of all the things that can go wrong at parties. Use this list to make a description of **your** disastrous party, using *too*, *too much*, *too many*, *too little*, *too few*, or *not enough*. Share your description with the rest of the class and decide who had the "worst" possible party.

meaning

FOCUS 4	*Too* versus *Very*

EXAMPLES	EXPLANATIONS
(a) *This writing is small.*	*Very* adds emphasis, but *too* shows that something is more than is necessary or desirable.
(b) *This writing is very small.*	In (b) the writing is small, but I can read it.
	In (c) the writing is smaller and I cannot read it.
(c) *This writing is too small.*	In these situations, *too* shows that you are unable to do something, but *very* does not.

EXERCISE 6

Complete the following with *too, too + to,* or *very,* as appropriate.

A: Hi Pam! I haven't seen you for ages!

B: I'm sorry. I've been (1) *too* busy *to* call. I've been house-hunting.

A: Did you find anything yet?

B: Yes, I found a place downtown. It's (2) _____ expensive, but I think I'll have enough money.

A: What was wrong with your old apartment?

B: I need a place where I can work on my art designs, and my old apartment was (3) _____ dark _____ work in. This apartment is (4) _____ large and sunny.

A: It sounds great. The problem with my apartment is that it's (5) _____ noisy. But it's also (6) _____ cheap, so I guess I'll stay there till I have some more money. Do you need any help moving?

B: Oh yes, please. Could you bring your car? My car is (7) _____ small _____ carry all my stuff. Afterwards we can go out for lunch together.

A: Yes, I'd like that (8) _____ much.

Complete the following with *very, too, too + to, enough, not enough,* or *too much/many/little/ few,* as appropriate.

Dear Tom and Wendy,

I'm writing to answer your questions about life in New York. In fact, this is quite hard to do because my opinions keep changing!

My apartment is nice, but the rent is (1) _____*very*_____ high. Luckily, I earn a good salary and I can afford it. The main problem is that the apartment just is (2) _____ big _____ I had to sell about half my furniture because I didn't have (3) _____ room for everything. I can't invite people for dinner because the kitchen is (4) _____ small _____ eat in. Luckily, the apartment has lots of windows, so all my plants are getting (5) _____ light. I live (6) _____ close to a subway station; it only takes me a couple of minutes to walk there. However, I never take the subway to work because it's (7) _____ crowded. You wouldn't believe it! There are just (8) _____ people crammed in like sardines, and you can't breathe because there is (9) _____ air. I haven't had the courage to ride my bike yet because there's just (10) _____ traffic. Mostly I walk everywhere, so the good news is that I am getting (11) _____ exercise!

Despite all this, there are lots of wonderful things about living here. There are (12) _____ museums and art galleries to keep me happy for years! However, at the moment, I have (13) _____ time to enjoy them because my job is driving me crazy. It's impossible to get all the work done because there are (14) _____ projects and (15) _____ good people to work on them. As a result, I am (16) _____ busy to make new friends or meet people. I don't sleep (17) _____ and so I am always tired. Worst of all, I don't even have (18) _____ time to stay in touch with dear old friends like you! Nevertheless, I'm certain things will get better soon. Why don't you come and visit? That would really cheer me up!

Love,

Mary

Use Your English

ACTIVITY 1 speaking

Work with a partner or in teams to play this version of tic-tac-toe.

■ **STEP 1** Decide who will be "X" and who will be "O" and toss a coin to see who will start the game.

■ **STEP 2** For each round of the game, select a different topic from the list below.

■ **STEP 3** Choose the square you want to start with. With your team, agree on a meaningful sentence expressing the idea written in the square and relating to the topic of the round. For example: TOPIC: This classroom. *"This classroom is very small," "There aren't enough chairs in this classroom," "There are too few windows in this classroom,"* and so on. If your sentence is correct, mark the square with "X" or "O".

■ **STEP 4** The first team to get three across, down, or diagonally is the winner.

TOPICS

1. This campus
2. Television
3. North America
4. This town or city

very	too + to	too
too few	not enough	too much
enough	too many	too little

ACTIVITY 2 writing

Write a letter to your local city councilor or mayor about a problem in your city or neighborhood. Describe the problem, and say why it is important. Be sure to use *too, enough,* and *very.* Suggest a possible solution.

■ **STEP 1** Look at the chart below. If you were responsible for making the laws in your community, at what ages would you permit the following activities? Write the ages in the column marked *Ideal Age.*

■ **STEP 2** Go around the room and collect information from your classmates about the ages at which these activities are permitted in the parts of the world (countries, states, provinces) that they know about. You can include information about this country (or state or province) as well. Write this in the last column.

ACTIVITY	IDEAL AGE	REAL AGE/WHERE
drive a car		
drink alcohol		
vote		
join the military		
get married		
own a gun		
leave school		

■ **STEP 3** When you have collected the information, prepare a report (oral or written) on the differences and similarities you found among different parts of the world. Include your own opinions about the ideal ages for these activities and give reasons to support them. Remember to announce the purpose of your report in your introduction and to end with a concluding statement. You can use these headings to organize your information: Introduction: Purpose of this report, Most interesting similarities among parts of the world, Most interesting differences among parts of the world, Your opinions on ideal ages, with reasons to support them, and Brief concluding statement.

■ **STEP 4** If you make a written report, remember to read it through carefully after you finish writing. Check to see if you were able to use any of the language in this unit. If you make an oral report, record your presentation and listen to it later. Write down any sentences that you used containing *too, very*, not enough, or *enough.*

ACTIVITY 4 speaking

The purpose of this activity is to share opinions on different social issues. Work with a partner and look at the issues listed below. For each one, think about what is sufficient (enough), what is insufficient (not enough), and what is excessive (too much) in this country and in other countries you and your partner know about. For example, you might think that public transportation in this country is too expensive and that there is not enough of it, but that public transportation in Egypt is very inexpensive but too slow. Record your opinions in your notebook. Be ready to share your ideas with the rest of the class.

Public Transportation   Housing

Health Care   Employment

Law and Order   Access for Disabled People to Public

Education   Buildings and Transportation

Care of the Elderly

ACTIVITY 5 writing

Choose **one** of the social issues you discussed in Activity 4. Review the information you collected on different countries. In your opinion, which country has the best solution? Which country, in your opinion, is the least successful in dealing with this issue? Write a short report, describing the best and worst solutions. Give reasons to support your opinions. Remember to introduce your topic; we have suggested one possibility below, but you can probably think of a better way. When you finish writing, read your report carefully and check to see if you were able to include any of the language discussed in this unit.

In the modern world, many countries are trying to find solutions to the same social issues, and it is interesting to see that different countries and cultures deal with these issues in different ways. In my opinion, some countries have better solutions than others. To illustrate this point, I will talk about _____ (social issue) and show how _____ (country) and _____ (country) both deal with it.

ACTIVITY 6 speaking/listening

■ **STEP 1** Use the information from Activity 4. As a class, choose four topics that interest you. Then, by yourself or with another student, interview a friend or another student about these topics. Record your interview. Listen to your recording and make a brief summary of the person's opinions. Share your findings with others. What similarities and differences did your class find in these interviews?

■ **STEP 2** Listen to your recording again and write down any sentences containing examples of language discussed in this unit.

ACTIVITY 7 listening

■ **STEP 1** List three serious problems facing the environment today.

■ **STEP 2** Listen to the audio of two people discussing environmental problems. Which opinions do you agree or disagree with and why?

CD Track 14

■ **STEP 3** Listen to the audio again. Write down as many phrases containing *too*, *enough*, and *very* as you can.

ACTIVITY 8 research on the web

InfoTrac® College Edition: What are the causes of world hunger? Why do some countries have too much food, and others not enough? Go to *InfoTrac* and search using the keywords 'causes of hunger'. What are the different ways this topic can be understood and explained? Make notes and present your ideas to the class.

ACTIVITY 9 reflection

What do you like and dislike about your classroom or library? What do you have too much/many of? What do you have too little/too few of? Tell your partner.

GIVING ADVICE AND EXPRESSING OPINIONS
Should, Ought To, Need To, Must, Had Better, Could, and Might

- Use *must, had better, need to, should, ought to, could, might,* and imperatives to give advice appropriately

- Use *should, ought to,* and *should not* to express opinions

OPENING TASK
How to . . .

In North America, many "self-improvement" or "self-help" books are published every year. These books give people advice on how to improve their lives.

■ ### STEP 1

With a partner, look at the titles of the books below. What kinds of advice do you expect to find in each one? Make up short dialogs about each book, similar to the example below.

Example:

Student A: *I need to learn about a healthy diet.*

Student B: *You should read* Live Longer, Eat Better.

■ ### STEP 2

Now read the sample passages from these books and match each one to the book you think it probably comes from.

A

As an important first step, you really ought to eliminate red meat. This may be hard at first, but you will be amazed to find that there are many healthy— and delicious—alternatives. *Live longer Eat Better.*

B

This is never as easy as it sounds, so you should be prepared to put time and effort into it. For example, doing volunteer work is one way to meet people who share your interests, and you may get to know them better as you work on projects together. *"Make More Friends"*

C

It's easier than you think. To really make a difference, you should start slowly and establish a routine. Think about one thing that you can easily do (carpool? recycle paper, cans, and glass?) As soon as this becomes a habit, you should start to think about what to do next. *x/days to Save the Planet.*

D

You should never settle into a regular, predictable routine. Surprise each other with fun activities, like picnics after work or moonlight barbecues on the beach. *How to Stay Marked.*

E

You ought to make every effort to motivate yourself to stay on your diet! Buy a dress that is just a little bit too small for you and hang it in your closet. You should look at it every day and dream of the time when it will really fit you. *Losing 30 Pounds in 30 days.*

F

You shouldn't draw attention to yourself. Choose conservative but attractive styles. Navy blue is a good color choice. Remember that you ought to look competent and professional at all times. *How to Dress for Success.*

■ **STEP 3**

With your partner, choose one of these self-help books. What advice would you give on the topic? Come up with at least three pieces of advice. Write these in your notebook.

FOCUS 1	Giving Advice with *Should, Ought To, Shouldn't*

EXAMPLES	EXPLANATIONS
(a) A: I'm so tired. B: You **should/ought to** get more sleep. (b) A: I can't understand my teacher. B: You **ought to/should** talk to her about it.	*Should/should not* and *ought to* are often used to give advice (to tell someone what you think is a good or bad idea for him or her to do). Use *should* or *ought to* to show that you think something is a good idea. *Ought to* is often pronounced as *oughta* in spoken English.
(c) A: I have a terrible cough. B: You **should not (shouldn't)** smoke so much.	Use *should not (shouldn't)* to show that you think something is a bad idea. *Ought to* is not usually used in negatives or in questions in American English.
(d) Nami works too hard. She **should/ought to** take a vacation. (e) NOT: She shoulds/oughts to take a vacation.	*Should* and *ought to* are modal auxiliaries. They do not take third person *s*. For more information about the form of modals, see Unit 5.

EXERCISE 1

Look at the advice that you and your partner wrote in the Opening Task on page 151. Did you use *should, ought to, should not*? Check to see if you used them correctly. If you didn't use them at all, rewrite your advice to include them.

Share your advice with the rest of the class. Do not tell your classmates which book you were thinking about when you wrote the advice and see if they can guess correctly.

FOCUS 2

Using *Need To* and Imperatives to Give Advice

EXAMPLES	EXPLANATIONS
(a) A: My tooth hurts. B: You **need to** see a dentist. (b) A: My tooth hurts. B: You **should/ought to** see a dentist.	*Need to* + base verb can also be used to give advice. It is stronger than *should* or *ought to*. *Need to* is not a modal verb.
(c) A: My tooth hurts. B: **Go** to a dentist. (d) A: I can't sleep. B: **Don't drink** so much coffee! (e) A: I can't sleep. B: You **shouldn't** drink so much coffee.	You can also use an imperative to give advice. An imperative is much stronger and much more direct than *need to*. If you do not know the person you are addressing very well, it is usually better to use *should/shouldn't* or *ought to*.

EXERCISE 2

Thompson Heinle ELT,
A Thompson Learning Company

We are proud to announce an exciting new book,
by language learners *for* language learners:

HOW TO BE A BETTER LANGUAGE LEARNER

Language learners from all over the world give you advice about ways to learn a second, third, or fourth language. This book will change the way you learn languages . . .

THOMSON
HEINLE

Australia · Canada · Mexico · Singapore · Spain · United Kingdom · United States

You have been asked to contribute to this exciting new "self-help" book. First, think about your own experience as a language learner. Then, in your notebook write down at least three important things that you think someone who wants to learn **your** language should or should not do. Get together with a partner and compare your lists. How many similarities and differences can you find in your advice? Share your advice with the rest of the class.

(fluttering your eyelashes)

use

FOCUS 3 — *Should* and *Ought To* versus *Must*

EXAMPLES	EXPLANATIONS
(a) **Alma:** I can't sleep at night. **Bea:** You **should** drink a glass of milk before you go to bed.	*Should* and *ought to* shows that something is a good idea. In (a), Bea is giving advice, but Alma is not obliged to follow that advice; she is free to do what she pleases.
(b) **Dora:** Do I need to get a special visa to visit Taiwan? **Wen:** Yes, you **must** go to the Taiwanese consulate here and get one before you leave. You **must not** try to enter the country without one.	*Must* is stronger. In (b), it is obligatory for Dora to follow Wen's advice. She is not free to do what she pleases. For more information about this use of *must*, see Unit 11.

■ EXERCISE 3

Oscar has just bought a used car. Complete the following, using *should, shouldn't, must,* or *must not* as appropriate. Different people may have different opinions about some of these, so be ready to justify your choices.

1. He _____should_____ get insurance as soon as possible.
2. He _____should / must._____ take it to a reliable mechanic and have it checked.
3. He _____must_____ get it registered.
4. He _____shouldn't / must not_____ drive it without insurance.
5. He _____must not_____ drink and drive.
6. He _____must_____ wear a seat belt.
7. He _____should_____ lock the doors when he parks the car.
8. He _____ought to_____ keep a spare key _(extra key)_ in a safe place.
9. He _____shouldn't_____ let other people drive his car.
10. He _____shouldn't_____ drive too fast.

use

| FOCUS 4 | *Should* and *Ought To* versus *Had Better* |

EXAMPLES	EXPLANATIONS
(a) You **should** go to all your classes every day. (b) You **had better** go to all your classes every day.	You can also use *had better* to give advice. *Had better* is much stronger than *should* and *ought to*, but not as strong as *must*. In (a), it is a good idea for you to do this. In (b), if you don't go, something bad will happen.
(c) You **should** see a doctor about that. (It's a good idea.) (d) You'**d better** see a doctor about that. (It's urgent.) (e) You **must** see a doctor about that. (It's obligatory.)	*Had better* often shows that you think something is urgent. *Had better* is often contracted to *'d better*.
(f) *Teacher to student:* If you want to pass this class, you **had better** finish all your assignments. (g) *Student to teacher:* If you come to my country, you **should** visit Kyoto. (h) NOT: You had better visit Kyoto.	*Had better* is often used in situations where the speaker has more power or authority (for example, boss to employee or teacher to student). In these situations, *had better* sounds like an order or a command. If you want to be sure that you sound polite, use *should* or *ought to*.
(i) You **had better** finish this tomorrow. (j) I **had better** leave now. (k) He **had better** pay me for this.	*Had better* refers to the present and the future. It does not refer to the past (even though it is formed with *had*).
(l) She'**d better not** tell anyone about this. (m) You'**d better not** be late.	Notice how the negative is formed.

EXERCISE 4

Angie is planning a trip to India and asks Sushila for some advice. Choose the most appropriate words from the box to complete the conversation. Use each word or phrase only once.

~~should~~   should not   ought to   must   'd better not   must not   'd better

Angie: I am planning a trip to India. Can you give me some advice?

Sushila: It's very hot there in the summer. You (1) ___should___ go there in January or February when the weather is cooler.

Angie: Do I need a visa?

Sushila: Yes, if you have a U.S. passport, you (2) ___must___ get a tourist visa. And you (3) ___had better___ get some vaccinations before you go. It's easy to get sick when you're not used to the food and water. You (4) ___ought to___ take some insect repellant and some stomach medicine, too.

Angie: What about money?

Sushila: It's a good idea to change some money before you go and take your credit card, but you (5) ___Had better not___ keep your credit card and passport together. If you lose both, you'll be in trouble!

Angie: What kind of clothes do I need?

Sushila: Take some light clothes for the day. But it can be cool at night, so you (6) ___shouldn't___ forget to take a sweater and jacket, too.

Angie: Are there any special customs I should know about?

Sushila: Yes, you (7) ___must not___ wear shoes when you enter someone's home.

EXERCISE 5

Circle your choice in each of the following sentences.

1. You (should not/**must not**) smoke when you are in a movie theater in the United States.

2. While you are in Los Angeles, you (**had better**/should) try to visit Disneyland.

3. In the state of Michigan, people under the age of 21 (should not/**must not**) try to purchase alcohol.

4. You ('d better not/must not) talk on your cell phone while you are driving in New York City; it's against the law!

5. You ('d better not/must not) take your car into downtown New York, because you may not find a parking space.

6. Everybody who comes into the United States (must/should) show a valid passport or picture ID.

7. If you are interested in Egyptian art, you (should/had better) visit the Metropolitan Museum in New York. They have a fantastic collection.

8. It's difficult to find a hotel room in Boston. We (must/should) make a reservation before we go there.

9. You (had better/should) visit Washington DC in the spring because the cherry trees are very beautiful at that time of year.

10. You (must/should) have an appointment before you can visit the White House.

| FOCUS 5 | *Should* versus *Could* and *Might* |

use

EXAMPLES	EXPLANATIONS
(a) A: I heard there's a new movie playing in town. B: Yeah, you **should** see that movie. It's great. (b) A: I don't know what to do on Friday night. B: You **could** see a movie.	You can also use *could* to give advice. *Could* is not as strong as *should* because it only expresses choices or possibilities. *Could* does not show that the speaker thinks that something is a good idea to do or that it is the right thing to do.
(c) If you want to improve your Spanish, you **could** take classes, you **might** listen to Spanish-speaking stations on the radio, you **could** find a conversation partner, or you **might** take a vacation in Mexico.	We often use *could* or *might* to express many different possibilities, without saying which one we think is best.

EXERCISE 6

Your friends always come to you when they have problems because you usually have lots of great ideas about what to do.

STEP 1 For each problem, write down as many possible solutions as you can think of, using *could* and *might*.

STEP 2 Get together with two or three other students and compare your ideas. Decide who has the best solution to each problem and write it down, using *should*.

Example: Your neighbors play loud rock music all night.

Possibilities: You could talk with them. You could play very loud opera in the morning when they are still asleep. You might move. You might buy earplugs. You could call the police.

In our opinion, the best solution: You should buy earplugs.

1. Your friend's husband snores. Possibilities: _____
_____

In our opinion, the best solution: _____
_____

2. Your friend's father is planning to come and visit for a few days. Unfortunately, he is a heavy smoker and your friend's roommates are nonsmokers who do not permit smoking in the house. Possibilities: _____
_____

In our opinion, the best solution: _____
_____

3. A classmate has just spilled coffee on her favorite white shirt. She doesn't know what to do. Possibilities: _____
In our opinion, the best solution: _____
_____

4. Your friend can't sleep at night. She feels exhausted every morning and doesn't have enough energy to do anything all day. Possibilities: _____
_____

In our opinion, the best solution: _____
_____

5. One of your classmates wants to learn more about American culture and customs and would really like to make friends with some Americans. He doesn't know how to start. You have lots of ideas. Possibilities: _____
_____

In our opinion, the best solution: _____
_____

6. Your partner never has enough money. At the end of the month, he is always broke. He comes to you for some ideas about what to do. Possibilities: _____

In our opinion, the best solution: _____

7. Two of your friends are taking a university class. The professor speaks very fast and they find it hard to follow the lectures. They are afraid that they are going to flunk the class. Possibilities: _____

In our opinion, the best solution: _____

8. Your friend's fiancée has two dogs. She has had these dogs since she was a child and is very attached to them. Unfortunately, your friend is allergic to dogs. He loves his fiancée very much, but the dogs are making him sick. He doesn't want to upset her. Possibilities: _____

In our opinion, the best solution: _____

▮ EXERCISE 7

The following story is a well-known logic problem. Get together with some of your classmates and decide on the best solution.

A woman went shopping. First she bought a large piece of cheese. Next she walked to a pet store where she bought a white mouse for her nephew's birthday. Just as she was leaving the store, she saw an adorable black and white cat. She couldn't leave the store without it, so she bought the cat as well.

Unfortunately, her car is parked a long way from the pet store, and it's only possible for her to carry one thing at a time. What could she do in order to get everything to her car? How many solutions can you find?

She could _____

There are no parking areas near the pet store, so she cannot move her car, and there is nobody around to help her. Unfortunately, cats eat mice and mice eat cheese. This means that if she leaves the cat with the mouse, the cat will eat the mouse, and if she leaves the mouse with the cheese, the mouse will eat the cheese. What should she do? What is the best solution to her problem?

She could _____

You can find the solution to this problem on page A-16.

There are many different versions of this problem. Do you know one? Share it with the rest of the class.

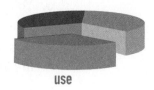

FOCUS 6

Should and Ought To versus Might, Could, Need To, Had Better, and Must

use

EXAMPLES	EXPLANATIONS
WEAK ↑ might could should/ought to need to had better ↓ must **STRONG**	All these verbs can be used to give advice. However, they express different degrees of strength.

EXERCISE 8

Read the following situation and follow the instructions given:

Jennifer is an American student. As she is planning to major in international business, she decided that it would be important for her to know how to speak Japanese. She managed to get some money from her father and left for Japan for six months.

She has now been in Tokyo for three months, taking classes in Japanese language and conversation. When she first arrived, she missed home a lot, so she quickly made friends with other Americans she met. Instead of living with a Japanese host family, she decided to move in with two other American women, and now she spends all her time with her new friends. She takes Japanese classes every day, but she seldom spends any time with the students who do not speak any English. As a result, she rarely speaks Japanese and has not made much progress in the language. She hasn't learned much about Japanese culture either.

Jennifer is having a great time in Tokyo with her American friends, but now she's in a terrible panic. Her father has just called to tell her that he will be coming to Tokyo on business, and he wants her to help him while he is there. He wants her to help interpret for him, as well as advise him on Japanese culture and customs. She is feeling very anxious about meeting her father. . . .

First, make a list of all the possible solutions to Jennifer's problem that you can think of in two minutes. Get together with another student and role-play a conversation with Jennifer. Then switch roles.

Example: You must try to meet some Japanese people.

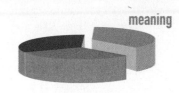

FOCUS 7	Expressing Opinions with *Should, Ought To,* and *Should Not*

EXAMPLES	EXPLANATIONS
(a) Iryna believes that more people **should** drive electric cars. (b) In Mune's opinion, more students **ought to** continue their education after high school. (c) Most of my friends think that we **shouldn't** eat meat.	You can also use *should, ought to,* and *should not* to express your opinions about what you think is right or wrong.

EXERCISE 9

In your opinion, which of the following occupations should receive the highest salaries? Number the occupations in order of the highest to the lowest salaries (Number 1 is the highest salary).

_____ TV news announcer	_____ CEO of a large company
_____ firefighter	_____ bus driver
_____ professional football player	_____ politician
_____ social worker	_____ elementary school teacher
_____ attorney	_____ plastic surgeon
_____ plumber	_____ police officer
_____ emergency room doctor	_____ nurse
_____ model	

When you finish, compare your answers with a partner's. Be ready to share and justify your opinions with the rest of the class.

Use Your English

ACTIVITY 1 speaking/listening

■ **STEP 1** Sometimes, for fun, people give each other advice on the best way to accomplish a negative goal—for example, the best way to lose your job or how to annoy your neighbors. Get together with another student and choose one of the following humorous topics. How many different ideas can you come up with?

- How to get a traffic ticket
- How to get rid of your boyfriend or girlfriend
- How to avoid learning English
- How to get an F in this class
- How to annoy your roommate

■ **STEP 2** With your partner, make a poster presentation on the topic you chose. Display your poster and use it to explain your ideas to the rest of the class.

■ **STEP 3** Record yourself as you make your poster presentation. Listen to your recording and write down all the sentences where you used *should, shouldn't, ought to, need to, must, had better, might,* or *could.* Did you use them appropriately?

ACTIVITY 2 speaking

Many American newspapers have advice columns. People write to these columns for help with their problems. Three famous ones are "Dear Abby," "Ann Landers," and "Miss Manners." Clip any advice columns you can find in various newspapers and bring them to class. Cut off the answers to the letters and circulate the letters without their replies. (But do not throw away the replies.) In groups, try to come up with helpful advice. Share your responses with the rest of the class. Compare your advice with the advice the professionals gave.

ACTIVITY 3 writing

In groups, write a letter to "Dear Abby," asking for advice on a particular problem. Exchange your problem letter with another group and write solutions to their problem. Share both problem and solution with the rest of the class.

ACTIVITY 4 writing

Write a short report, giving advice to someone who is planning to visit your hometown, your country, or the community where you grew up. Advise him or her on places to visit, clothes to wear, things to bring, things to do, and how to act.

Remember to start your report with an introductory statement.

Example: My hometown/country, (name), is very interesting, and if you follow my advice, I am sure that you will have an enjoyable and rewarding visit. . . .

When you finish writing, check and see if you have used *should, shouldn't, must, ought to, might, need to, could,* and *had better.* It is not necessary to use one in every sentence, as this would sound very unnatural!

ACTIVITY 5 speaking

Is honesty always the best policy? Should we **always** tell the truth? Think about the following situations. Share your opinions on each one with your classmates. How many people share your point of view? How many have different ideas?

1. You saw your best friend's girlfriend out on a date with someone else. Should you tell your friend what you saw? Why? Why not?

2. A classmate cheated on the last test. Should you tell your teacher? Why? Why not?

3. Your friend has a new haircut. She is really happy with her new "look," but you don't like it at all. In fact, you think it makes her look quite ugly. She asks for your opinion. Should you tell her what you really think? Why? Why not?

4. You catch your 8-year-old son telling a lie. Should you tell him that it is wrong to lie? Why? Why not?

ACTIVITY 6 speaking/writing

STEP 1 Read the following and circle *should* or *should not* to express the point of view that is closest to your own opinion on the topic.

1. School uniforms should/should not be obligatory.

2. Animals should/should not be used in laboratory experiments.

3. Doctors should/should not reveal the identity of an AIDS patient to the patient's employer or school.

4. Mothers should/should not work outside the home while their children are young.

5. A woman should/should not take her husband's family name when she marries.

6. Smoking should/should not be permitted in public places.

STEP 2 Choose the topic that interests you the most and then go around the room until you find one or two other students who share your opinion on that topic. Form a group with these students and brainstorm all the reasons and examples you can think of to support your point of view and then write them down. Choose the strongest ones, with the best examples, and use them to make a short report (oral or written) presenting your opinion. Share your report with the rest of the class and be ready to justify your position as necessary.

STEP 3 If you make a written report, read your report carefully and underline every example you can find of the modal auxiliaries from this unit.

If you choose an oral report, record your report. Listen to your recording and write down every sentence where you use one of the modal auxiliaries from this unit.

ACTIVITY 7 listening

CD Track 15

In this activity, you will hear an interview on the topic of smoking. Listen to the person's opinion. Does she think smoking should be banned in public places? What other ideas does she express? Check (✓) the statements you think the speaker agrees with.

_____ Smoking should be banned in public places.

_____ People should not be able to buy cigarettes in drugstores and supermarkets.

_____ Parents should not smoke at home in front of children.

_____ Teachers need to teach students about the dangers of smoking.

Listen to the audio again. Write down any sentences that contain examples of the verb forms in this unit.

ACTIVITY 8 speaking/listening

Many people have strong opinions about smoking. Ask five different people questions like these: "What's your opinion about smoking in public places?" "Do you think it's a good or bad idea to ban smoking in public places?"

Record their answers. Listen to your recording and be ready to share the information that you collect with the other people in your class. What do most of the people you interviewed think about this topic?

Listen to your recordings again. What are some of the words and the ways people used to express their opinions? Write down any sentences that contain examples of the verbs from this unit.

ACTIVITY 9 research on the web

InfoTrac® College Edition: Go to *InfoTrac* and search articles for advice on how to stop smoking. Type keywords "how to stop smoking." Take notes of the main points. What do you think should be done to stop people from smoking? Discuss this issue with your class.

ACTIVITY 10 reflection

What problems do you have studying English? Write down three problems. Tell your partner and ask for some advice.

MODALS OF NECESSITY AND PROHIBITION

Have To/Have Got To, Do Not Have To, Must/Must Not, Cannot

- Use *must*, *have to*, and *have got to* to show something is necessary

- Use *must not* and *cannot* to show something is prohibited

- Choose between *have to* and *have got to*

- Use *do not have to* to show something is not necessary

- Use *have to* for *must* in the past

OPENING TASK

Customs and Immigration

■ STEP 1

Every country has rules about what you can bring with you when you enter the country. What is one rule you must follow to enter the United States? What is one rule you must follow to enter the country you are from?

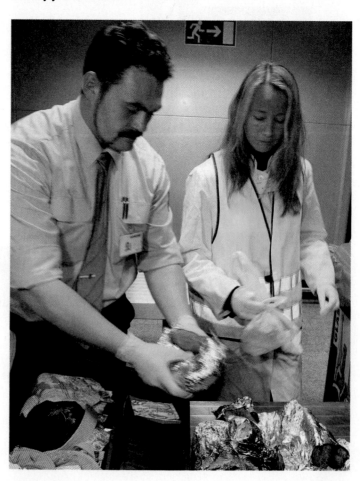

STEP 2

A friend of yours in Taiwan is planning a short vacation to California. He doesn't have much room to pack a lot of things because he's planning to travel with just a backpack. Here are some of the things he is thinking of taking with him:

a passport (1)
a surfboard (3)
fresh fruit (1)(2)
an international driver's
    license (3)
traveler's checks (3)
books about China (4)
a return airline ticket (1)

a map of the United States (3)
fireworks (2)
a laptop computer (3) or (4)
a credit card (3)(1)
a tourist visa (1)
California guide books (3)
photographs of his
    hometown (4)

an umbrella (4)
a business suit (3)(4)
hiking boots (4)
a cell phone (3)
Chinese pop music CDs (4)

STEP 3

Use the box below to help your friend organize the things he wants to take to the United States. Work with a partner and put them in the category where you think they belong.

1. It's necessary and obligatory: You can't enter the United States without this: You must take this with you.	3. It's a good idea to bring this: You should take this with you.
2. It's prohibited by law: You must not take this into the United States.	4. It's O.K. to bring this, but it isn't really necessary: You don't have to take this.

STEP 4

With your partner, write sentences about one or two items in each category, explaining why you think they belong there.

FOCUS 1 | Modals of Necessity, Prohibition, and Permission

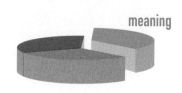

EXAMPLES	EXPLANATIONS
(a) You **must** have a passport. OR (b) You **have to** have a passport. OR (c) You **have got to** have a passport.	Use *must, have to,* or *have got to* to show something is necessary and obligatory (something that is strongly required, often by law).
(d) You **must not (mustn't)** bring fresh fruit into the United States. OR (e) You **cannot (can't)** bring fresh fruit into the United States.	Use *must not (mustn't)* or *cannot (can't)* to show something is prohibited and absolutely not permitted (often by law).
(f) When I traveled to Iceland last year, **I couldn't** take any meat products.	In the past, use *couldn't.*
(g) If you go to live in Japan next year, you **won't be able to** take any pets with you.	In the future, use *will not (won't)* be able to.
(h) You **can** bring a surfboard.	Use *can* to show that something is permitted.
(i) About ten years ago, you **could** smoke on an airplane.	In the past, use *could.*
(j) In the future, you **will be able to** go to bed on an airplane.	In the future, use *will be able to.*
(k) You **should** bring a credit card.	Use *should* to show something is a good idea. For more information about this use of *should* see Unit 10.
(l) You **don't have** to bring a surfboard.	Use *do not (don't) have to* to show something is permitted, but not necessary. You can do this if you want to, but you are not required to.

EXERCISE 1

Look back at the sentences you wrote in Step 4 of the Opening Task. Did you use *must, have to, have got to, should, can, can't, mustn't,* and *don't have to*? If you did, check to see that you used them correctly. If you didn't use them, rewrite the sentences.

Example: *He must have a valid passport—it is required by law.*

In the rest of this unit, you will have the opportunity to practice all of these in more detail.

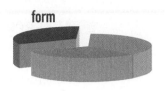
form

Modals and Phrasal Modals: *Must, Have To*, and *Have Got To*

EXAMPLES	EXPLANATIONS
(a) International students **must** get visas before they enter the United States.	*Must* is a modal and does not change to agree with the subject.
(b) My Taiwanese friend **must** get a tourist visa before he goes to the United States on vacation.	
(c) International students **have to** get visas before they enter the United States.	*Have to* is a phrasal modal. It changes to agree with the subject.
(d) My Taiwanese friend **has to** get a tourist visa before he goes on vacation in the United States.	*Have to* and *has to* are usually pronounced "hafta" and "hasta" in fast speech and informal conversation.
(e) International students **have got to** get visas before they enter the United States.	*Have got to* is a phrasal modal. It changes to agree with the subject.
(f) My Taiwanese friend **has got to** get a tourist visa before he goes to the United States on vacation.	*Have got to* and *has got to* are usually pronounced " 've gotta" and " 's gotta" in fast speech and informal conversation.
(g) **Do** we **have to** go? **Does** she **have to** go too?	Notice how questions with *must, have to,* and *have got to* are formed. Use *do/does* with *have to.*
(h) **Have** we **got to** go? **Has** she **got to** go too?	Use *has/have* with *have got to.* Do not use *do/does.*
(i) **Must** we go? **Must** she go too?	Do not use *do/does* with *must.* However, *must* is rarely used in questions in American English.

Many road signs are used internationally, but some used in the United States are confusing for tourists from other countries. What do you think the following road signs mean? Complete the sentences, using *have to* and *have got to* in your answers.

1.  In the United States, drivers _have to turn right._ when they see this sign.

2.  Also, when they see this one, they _have to come to a complete stop._

3. 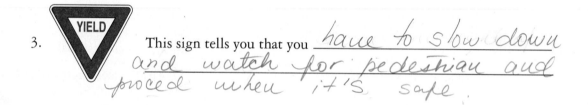 This sign tells you that you _have to slow down and watch for pedestrian and proced when it's safe._

4.  A driver who sees this sign _have to slow down and watch for pedestrian who are crossing._

5. 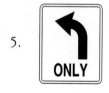 Be careful when you see this one. It means that you _only have to turn left._

6. Q: What happens when there are two or three cars waiting at this sign?
   A: The car that arrives last _have to wait they turn._

How many of these road signs on page 170 are also found in your country? Are there are any road signs from your country that are not found in North America? Draw the signs and write sentences showing what you have to do when you see them.

EXERCISE 3

Work with a partner and decide which of the following are necessary and obligatory to do if you want to get a driver's license in the United States.

speak English very well

take driving lessons ✓

practice before the test

take an eye test ✓

take a written test ✓

have a medical examination

have a passport or birth certificate as ID ✓

pass a driving test ✓

have a high school diploma

own a car

study the information booklet from the ✓ DMV (Department of Motor Vehicles, the department that issues driver's licenses)

have an international driver's license

EXERCISE 4

Role-play this situation with your partner. Your friend will ask you questions about how to get a driver's license. Answer the questions and explain what is necessary to get a driver's license in the United States; then explain what is necessary to get a driver's license in the country you are from. Then switch roles.

Example: A: *Do I have to take a written test?*

B: *Yes, you have to take a written test and a driving test.*

FOCUS 3 — *Have To* versus *Have Got To*

use

EXAMPLES	EXPLANATIONS
(a) Joe **has to** go on a diet.	Both *have to* and *have got to* show that something is necessary and obligatory. However, many people use *have got to* when they want to emphasize that something is **very** important and **very** necessary.
(b) Joe **has got to** follow a very strict diet because he has a serious heart condition. (If he doesn't follow the diet, he will die.)	
(c) You **have to** pay your phone bill once a month.	
(d) You **have got to** pay your phone bill immediately. (If you don't, the phone company will disconnect the phone.)	
(e) Hey Steve, **you've got to (gotta)** see this movie. It's really great.	In very informal conversation among friends, some people use *have got to* to show they think something is a really good thing to do. In (e), Steve's friend is not saying that Steve is obliged to see the movie; she is just strongly advising Steve to see it.

■ EXERCISE 5

Make a statement for each situation. Work with a partner and decide which you would use for each one: *have to* or *have got to*.

1. Your sister's 4-year-old son takes a nap every day and goes to bed at 8:00 every night. But today he didn't take a nap, and it's now 10:00 P.M.

   She says to her son, "You _____ go to sleep now."

2. The last time your friend went to the dentist was four years ago. He doesn't think he has any problems with his teeth, but he feels he should probably go to the dentist for a checkup.

   He says, "I _____ make an appointment to see the dentist sometime soon."

3. You haven't been reading the assignments for your history class, and you did very badly on the first two quizzes. You are afraid that you'll fail the course.

   You tell your classmate, "I _____ study every day if I don't want to fail my history class."

4. Your roommate is making dinner. She has just put a loaf of bread in the oven. Suddenly she realizes that she doesn't have an important item that she needs for dessert.

She says, "I _____ go to the store. If I'm not back in ten minutes, can you take the bread out of the oven? It _____ come out at 7:00 or it'll be ruined."

5. You are at a friend's house. You are feeling a little tired and want to go to sleep early.

You say, "I _____ leave now. I'll see you after class tomorrow."

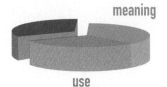

meaning

use

FOCUS 4	Using *Cannot* (*Can't*) and *Must Not* (*Mustn't*) to Show Something Is Prohibited or Not Permitted

EXAMPLES	EXPLANATIONS
(a) You **cannot (can't)** bring fresh fruit into the United States. OR (b) You **must not (mustn't)** bring fresh fruit into the United States. (c) You **cannot (can't)** smoke in here. OR (d) You **must not (mustn't)** smoke in here.	Use *cannot* and *must not* to show that something is completely prohibited or not permitted (often by law). *Cannot* is more common than *must not* in American English. *Cannot* and *must not* are usually contracted to *can't* and *mustn't* in fast speech.
(e) Herbert, you **must not (mustn't)** eat any more of those cookies!	*Must not/mustn't* is also often used as a strong command in situations where you want someone to obey. In (e), eating cookies is not prohibited by law, but the speaker **really** wants Herbert to stop eating them.

EXERCISE 6

Look at the cartoon. Write statements in your notebook that use *cannot* and *must not* to describe each prohibited activity.

EXERCISE 7

Where would you see each of the signs below? Match the signs with the places. Say what you *can, must, cannot,* or *must not* do there. (Some signs may be found in more than one place.)

airport   museum   movie theater

supermarket   restaurant   school

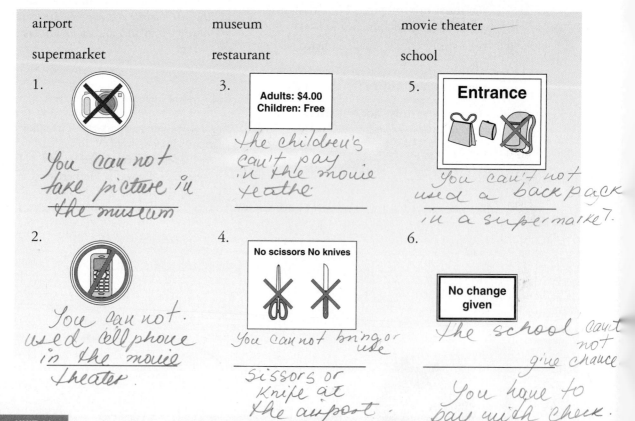

1.

You can not take picture in the museum

2.

You can not. used cellphone in the moure theater.

3. **Adults: $4.00** **Children: Free**

the children's can't pay in the moure yeathe.

4. **No scissors No knives**

You cannot bring or use sissors or knife at the aupoot.

5. **Entrance**

You can't not used a back pack in a supermarke7.

6. **No change given**

the school can't not give chance You have to pay with check.

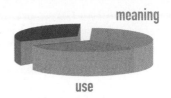

meaning

use

FOCUS 5	*Must* and *Have To* versus *Must Not, Cannot,* and *Do Not Have To*

EXAMPLES	EXPLANATIONS
(a) To enter the United States you **must** have a valid passport. OR (b) To enter the United States you **have to** have a valid passport.	Showing something is necessary and obligatory: Use either *must* or *have to.* In this situation, they have the same meaning.
(c) You **cannot** bring fireworks into the United States. OR (d) You **must not** bring fireworks into the United States. (e) NOT: You don't have to bring fireworks into the United States.	Showing something is prohibited: Use *cannot* or *must not.* Do not use *do not have to.* In negative sentences, they do not have the same meaning. In this situation, *must not* means it is prohibited.
(f) You **don't have to** bring a surfboard to California because you can rent one there. (g) NOT: You must not bring a surfboard to California because you can rent one there. (h) There aren't any classes on Saturdays, so we **don't have to** come to school.	Showing something is not necessary: Use *do not have to.* Do not use *cannot* or *must not.* In this situation, *do not have to* means you can do something if you want to, but you are not obliged to do it if you don't want to.

EXERCISE 8

Look back at the places and signs in Exercise 7. Can you use *don't have to* to describe any of these signs?

EXERCISE 9

With your partner, make a list of rules for your classroom, using *must, must not, cannot,* and *don't have to.* Take a vote to see which ones your classmates want to put on your classroom walls. Draw signs to go with your rules.

Example: *You cannot smoke in this room.*

The magazine article below is about traffic laws in different European countries.

STEP 1 Before you read the article, look at the following statements. Do you think they are probably true or probably false? Circle T (for *true*), or F (for *false*). After you finish reading, look at the statements again and change your answers if necessary.

1. In Germany, you mustn't use bad language or make rude and insulting gestures if you get angry with other drivers.   T   F
2. You must be careful when you honk your horn in Greece.   T   F
3. You have to honk your horn when you pass another car in Gibraltar.   T   F
4. You cannot flash your lights at other drivers in Luxembourg.   T   F
5. In Scandinavian countries, you cannot drive with your headlights on during the day.   T   F
6. You have to drive more slowly at night in Austria.   T   F
7. In Romania, you don't have to keep your car clean.   T   F

How not to collide with local road laws

If you are planning on driving in Europe, you should know that driving laws and customs vary greatly from country to country.

Be careful not to allow frustration with other drivers to develop into swearing or offensive gestures in Germany: They are illegal. Displays of anger are not welcome in Greece, either.

It is unlawful to honk your horn too loudly (although this may surprise many visitors to Athens!). In Gibraltar, using your horn at all is completely prohibited. In Luxembourg, the law says that drivers have to flash their lights each time they pass another car.

In Scandinavian countries, you have to drive with your headlights dimmed during the day, but in Poland, this is obligatory only in winter.

Make sure you fill your tank before you get on the Autobahn in Germany: It is illegal to run out of gas. Speed limits vary too, not just from country to country, but within countries as well. Beware of speed limits that change from one moment to the next. For example, in Austria, speed limits are lower at night and in France, the speed limit on the freeways drops from 130 kmh* to 110 kmh when it rains. (And if the French police catch you speeding, you have to pay a massive on-the-spot fine!)

But perhaps the strangest law of all is from Romania, where you must not drive your car if it is dirty.

Adapted with permission from *The European* (Magazine Section), 6/9/95
*kmh = kilometers per hour

STEP 2 Make statements using *must, have to, cannot, mustn't,* or *do not have to* about the following topics from the article.

1. Driving in Poland during the winter: _____

_____

2. Driving on the Autobahn in Germany: _____

_____

3. Driving on the freeways in France: _____

_____

STEP 3 Are there any traffic laws that are sometimes confusing to visitors to the country you come from? Describe them to the rest of your class, using *must, have to, cannot, must not,* and *do not have to* where you can.

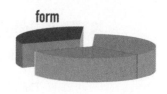

FOCUS 6

Talking about the Present, Past, and Future with *Have To* and *Must*

PRESENT	PAST	FUTURE
must	—	must
have to	had to	have to/will have to
do not have to	did not have to	do not have to/will not have to

EXAMPLES	EXPLANATIONS
(a) Students **have to** start school at 8:00 A.M. (b) Students **must** start school at 8:00 A.M. (c) Students **don't have to** go to school on Saturdays.	Use *must (not)*, *have to*, and *do not have to* to show that something is (or is not) necessary in the present.
(d) We **had to** stay late after school yesterday. (e) We **didn't have to** take the test last week.	Notice that there is no past tense form of *must* when it shows necessity. Use *had to* to show that something was necessary in the past.
(f) Ron **must** go to a meeting tomorrow. OR (g) Ron **has to** go to a meeting tomorrow. OR (h) Ron **will have to** go to a meeting tomorrow.	You can use *must*, *have to*, or *will have to* to talk about events that will be necessary in the near future.
(i) He **doesn't have to** go to school next week. (j) He **will not (won't) have to** go to school next week.	You can also use negative forms *do not have to* or *will not have to* to talk about the near future.

EXERCISE 11

Maggie and her friend Jan are talking about jobs. Maggie is describing a job she had last summer. Complete their conversation with *have to,* and *do not have to* in the present, past, or future.

Maggie: The worst job I ever had was last summer, when I worked as a waitress in that tourist restaurant down by the aquarium.

Jan: Oh really? What was so terrible about it?

Maggie: For a start, I (1) _____ get up at 5:00 A.M. and, as I didn't have a car then, I (2) _____ walk.

Jan: Why didn't you take the bus?

Maggie: It doesn't start running until 7:00, and I (3) _____ be at the restaurant by 6:30 to set the tables for breakfast.

Jan: That's tough. Did they make you wear a silly uniform or anything?

Maggie: No, thank goodness. We (4) _____ wear any special uniforms, except for hats. We all (5) _____ wear really stupid sailor caps. Mine was too small and it kept falling off.

Jan: So you're probably not planning on working there again next summer.

Maggie: Absolutely not. I'm earning twice as much at my present job, so with a bit of luck, I'll be able to save some money and I (6) _____ work at all next summer.

Jan: That sounds good. What's your present job like?

Maggie: It's much better. I start work at 11:00 A.M.

Jan: So you (7) _____ get up early. What about weekends?

Maggie: I (8) _____ work on weekends, but if I want to make some extra money, I can go in on Saturdays. It's ideal.

Jan: Maybe I should try to get a job there. Our landlord raised the rent last month and I just can't afford to stay there on my present salary.

EXERCISE 12

Read the letter and choose the correct answer for each blank from the list below.

Dear Kimberley,

It's almost the end of the school year and we are in the middle of final exams.
We (1) _____ take a lot of different tests and write essays. Luckily,
my grades in English language are quite good, so I (2) _____ take any
extra tests. Last year I (3) _____ go to summer school for two months
because my grades were so bad, but I hope I (4) _____ go this year.
My parents say I (5) _____ come to stay with you this summer unless
I pass all my classes.

It's getting late now and I (6) _____ finish writing this letter. I
have a history exam tomorrow morning and I (7) _____ go over all
my notes tonight. In middle school, we (8) _____ take our notes into
the exam, but here we (9) _____. I want to get a good average, so I
(10) _____ fail this exam. I'm looking forward to seeing you again
this summer. You (11) _____ write and tell me when I can come to
visit you. There's a new Johnny Depp movie coming out in July and we (12)
_____ go and see it together!

Love from,

Charlene

1. ○ (a) have got to   ○ (b) must not   ○ (c) have to
2. ○ (a) must not   ○ (b) couldn't   ○ (c) don't have to
3. ○ (a) had to   ○ (b) should   ○ (c) must
4. ○ (a) can't   ○ (b) won't have to   ○ (c) must not
5. ○ (a) must not   ○ (b) can't   ○ (c) don't have to
6. ○ (a) can   ○ (b) have to   ○ (c) had to
7. ○ (a) have got to   ○ (b) had to   ○ (c) could
8. ○ (a) can   ○ (b) should   ○ (c) could
9. ○ (a) couldn't   ○ (b) don't have to   ○ (c) can't
10. ○ (a) must not   ○ (b) don't have to   ○ (c) couldn't
11. ○ (a) had to   ○ (b) don't have to   ○ (c) must
12. ○ (a) can't   ○ (b) had to   ○ (c) have got to

Use Your English

ACTIVITY 1 speaking

In Exercises 2, 6, and 7 you saw some examples of signs. The local tourist board has asked you and your classmates to create some signs for tourists visiting the area. Get together with two or three other students and draw at least three signs. For example: *You must not feed the ducks. You must have exact change for the bus. You must not drink this water*. Draw each sign on a different piece of paper. Do not write anything next to the sign—your classmates must guess what it is. Look at their signs and write down what you think they mean.

ACTIVITY 2 speaking

In this activity, you will be comparing your childhood memories with those of your classmates. Think back to when you were a child. Write down five things you had to do then that you do not have to do now. Example for Childhood: I had to go to bed early. Then write down five things you did not have to do then that you have to do now. Example for Now: I can stay up late.

Next, compare your list with those of two or three other classmates and be ready to report on your findings to the rest of the class.

YOU		YOUR CLASSMATES	
Childhood	Now	Childhood	Now
1	1	1	1
2	2	2	2
3	3	3	3
4	4	4	4
5	5	5	5

ACTIVITY 3 writing

A friend of yours is interested in studying at a North American university. Write him or her a letter explaining what he or she will have to do in order to enter a university.

ACTIVITY 4 speaking/listening

CD Tracks
16,17,18

■ **STEP 1** Do you know what a person has to do in order to get any of the following?

- a green card (for permanent residence in the United States)
- a Social Security number
- a marriage license
- a credit card
- United States citizenship

With a partner, make a list of what you think a person must or has to do in order to get each of these.

■ **STEP 2** Listen to the audio. You will hear somebody discussing three of the above topics. Which topics are the speakers talking about? What do they think you have to do to get these things? Make notes in the chart below or in your notebook.

TOPIC	WHAT YOU HAVE TO DO
1	
2	
3	

■ **STEP 3** Now look at the list you and your partner made on the same topic. How many differences and how many similarities can you find?

■ **STEP 4** Listen to the audio again. Write down any sentences containing examples of modals and phrasal modals expressing necessity and prohibition. Refer to Focus 1 and Focus 2 for review of these modals.

ACTIVITY 5 speaking/listening

■ **STEP 1** Choose a topic from Activity 4 that you don't know anything about.

■ **STEP 2** Interview three different people and ask them what they know about the topic. For example, you can ask: *What does somebody have to do if they want to get a green card?*

Record your interviews. Listen to your recording and take notes. Did all the people you interviewed tell you the same information? Or did they tell you different things? Share your findings with the rest of your class.

■ **STEP 3** Listen to your recording again and write down any sentences containing *must, have to, must not, cannot, do not have to, have got to,* or *should.*

ACTIVITY 6 research on the web

On the Web: Use an Internet search engine such as Google® or Yahoo® to get more information about one of the topics in Activity 4. Take notes on what you read. Summarize your findings and tell the class. Be sure to make a note of which Web sites you used.

ACTIVITY 7 reflection

Make a list of helpful guidelines for a new student who is going to start studying English. Divide your list into things that are necessary things that are not necessary. Compare lists with a partner. What things did you need to do in the past that you do not need to do now?

EXPRESSING LIKES AND DISLIKES

French Fries.
Chips y papas fritas .or
Fries.

OPENING TASK

What Kind of Food Do You Like?

■ STEP 1

Work in a group. Name the different foods in the pictures. Which ones do you like most? Which ones do you dislike?

Bunp
tomatow
Meat.
letuce.
Pickles.
Mayonese.

(Hamburger).

Chese.
Cake. and
whipped.
Cream.

Breding

tarta Souce

Cathin
Board.

French Fries.
Chicken or Fish.
Salad.

Fruits:
Orange; kiwi.
Pineaple
grapes.

■ STEP 2

Work with a partner. One of you is A, the other is B. Talk about food that you like and don't like, and complete the chart on the next page together.

STEP 3

In the top left-hand box, write three kinds of food that A and B both like. In the top right-hand box, write three kinds of foods that A does not like, but B does. In the bottom left-hand box, write three kinds of food B doesn't like, but A does. In the last box, write three kinds of food that both A and B do not like.

		STUDENT A	
		LIKES	**DOESN'T LIKE**
STUDENT B	**LIKES**	(A likes, and B does, too.) - Pizza - Cake. - Pasta.	(A doesn't like, but B does.) - Chocolate - Beens. - Fish.
	DOESN'T LIKE	(B doesn't like, but A does.) - Papaya. - Mellou - Banana Fries (Brazilian Style) - tofu.	(B doesn't like, and A doesn't either.) - Pickles - whipped cream - Lamb. meat.

STEP 4

Share some of these findings with the class. Make a list of statements with *like* and *dislike* (or *doesn't/don't like*).

Example: *I like spicy food and Tina does too.*

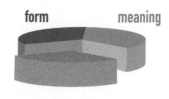
form   meaning

FOCUS 1   Expressing Similarity with *Too* and *Either*

EXAMPLES	EXPLANATIONS
(a) I like fruit, **and Roberta does too.** (b) NOT: I like fruit, and Roberta likes fruit.	To avoid repetition in affirmative sentences (sentences without *not*), use *and* (<u>X</u>) *do/does too.*
(c) Roberta doesn't eat meat, and I **don't either.** (d) NOT: I don't eat meat, and Roberta doesn't eat meat.	To avoid repetition in negative sentences (sentences with *not*), use *and* (<u>X</u>) *do/doesn't either.*

 ## EXERCISE 1

Check the statements you made in Step 4 of the Opening Task on page 185. Did you use *too* and *either* correctly? If not, rewrite these statements using *too* and *either.*

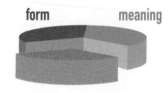
form   meaning

FOCUS 2   Expressing Similarity with *So* and *Neither*

EXAMPLES	EXPLANATIONS
(a) I like fruit, **and so does** Roberta. (b) Roberta doesn't eat meat, **and neither do I.**	Another way to avoid repetition is with *and so do/does* (<u>X</u>) in affirmative sentences, and with *and neither do/does* (<u>X</u>) in negative sentences. Invert subject and verb after *so* and *neither.*

EXERCISE 2

Now work with a different partner and share the information on your charts in the Opening Task. Use this information to complete the following report. Make sure that your statements are not only grammatical but also true.

My classmates and I have strong opinions about the kinds of food we like and dislike. For example, _____ and so

_____.

_____ and neither

_____.

_____ too.

_____ either.

    We also found other similarities in our taste in food. _____

either. _____

neither _____.

_____ so

_____. _____ too.

FOCUS 3   Expressing Similarity with *So*

use

EXAMPLES	EXPLANATIONS
(a) I speak French, and so **does** my mother. (b) My mother exercises every day, and so **do** I.	Use *do* when you do not want to repeat the verb. Make sure that there is subject/verb agreement: I *do* he/she *does* they/you *do*
(c) I **can** speak French, and so **can** she. (d) I **have** studied it, and so **has** she.	Use an auxiliary verb (*can, have, should*) if the first verb uses one.
(e) I **am** happy, and so **is** she.	Use a form of *be* if the first verb is a form of *be*.

Read Lucille's story about her friend Barbara. Match the first half of the sentences in column A with the second half in column B. Draw an arrow to show the connection. The first one has been done for you.

1. Barbara is 18 years old

2. Barbara went to Clarke High School

3. I didn't study very hard

4. She likes to travel

5. I can't drive

6. Barbara's job isn't interesting

7. She'll quit her job soon

8. Barbara's parents want to go to California

9. They don't have much money

10. Barbara has never been to California

11. Barbara has studied Spanish

12. We're excited about going to California

a. and neither do we.

b. and so have I.

c. and so will I.

d. and so am I.

e. and neither have I.

f. and so do my parents.

g. and I did too.

h. and Barbara didn't either.

i. and Barbara can't either.

j. and I do too.

k. and they are too.

l. and neither is mine.

use

FOCUS 4   Showing Agreement with Short Phrases

EXAMPLES

(a) **Tina:** I love going to movies.
    Rob: So do I.

(b) **Tina:** I never go to violent movies.
    Rob: Neither do I.

(c) **Tina:** I can't stand watching violence.
    Rob: I can't either.

(d) **Tina:** I prefer comedies.
    Rob: Really? I do too.

EXPLANATIONS

Short phrases such as *so do I, neither do I, I can't either,* and *I do too* are used to show agreement with somebody else's opinions and ideas. They are very common in informal conversation.

EXERCISE 4

Read the comic strip. Can you find the missing parts of the conversation in the list below? Write the letters in the appropriate cartoon bubble.

A. I don't either!

B. I do too!

C. Neither can I!

D. So did I!

E. Neither will I!

F. So is mine!

G. I will too!

H. So am I!

I. I can't either!

Short Phrases or Hedges and Emphatic *Do*

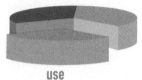

use

EXAMPLES	EXPLANATIONS
(a) **Sue:** I love ballet. What about you? **Tien:** Kind of. (b) **Sue:** Do you like opera? **Tien:** Sort of.	If you do not agree strongly with the speaker's opinions, you can use hedges (*sort of, kind of*) in informal conversation. In fast speech, *sort of* sounds like "sorta" and *kind of* sounds like "kinda."
(c) **Tien:** You really **are** a good swimmer. (d) **Sue:** Thanks! I **do** love swimming. (e) **Tien:** You know, I **really do** enjoy our conversations, Sue.	You can add emphasis to a sentence by stressing the auxiliary or the *be* verb. In sentences where there is no auxiliary or *be* verb, you can add *do* and stress it for emphasis. You can add extra emphasis by adding *really* or *certainly* before the auxiliary verb.

EXERCISE 5

Claire and Chris have just met at a party and are finding out how much they have in common. Look at the chart showing their likes and dislikes.

✓ ✓ ✓ = really a lot   ✓ ✓ = a lot   ✓ = a little

Use the information from the chart to complete the conversation. Use agreement phrases with *so* or *neither*, hedges, or emphatic structures with *really* or *certainly* where appropriate. The first one has been done for you.

	LIKES		DISLIKES
Chris	swimming ✓✓✓ cats ✓✓ cooking ✓✓	hiking ✓✓ music ✓ Chinese food ✓✓	TV ✓✓ getting up in the morning ✓✓✓ country music ✓✓
Claire	cats ✓ eating in restaurants ✓✓ Chinese food ✓✓✓	cooking ✓ music ✓✓ swimming ✓✓ hiking ✓	country music ✓✓✓ getting out of bed ✓✓ staying home ✓✓ watching TV ✓✓

Chris: Well, let me see . . . what are some of my favorite things? The ocean . . . I (1) _____really do_____ love swimming in the ocean.

Claire: (2) _____so Do I_____. Maybe we should go for a swim sometime.

Chris: Yes, that'd be great! Do you like hiking too?

Claire: (3) _____Sort of._____ In general, I prefer to be active. I mean I don't like sitting at home and watching TV.

Chris: (4) _____Neither Do I_____. But I (5) _____really don't_____ like getting up in the morning.

Claire: Well, (6) ___Me either___. [handwritten above: Neither Do I.] Most people don't like getting out of bed in the morning! What about music? Do you like music?

Chris: (7) ___Kind of___. I don't know too much about it, actually.

Claire: Really? I love all kinds of music, except for country. I hate country!

Chris: (8) ___Me too___. [handwritten below: I do too] We (9) ___Really___ do agree on that one! What else? I love cooking, don't you?

Claire: (10) ___Sort of___. I really prefer eating out in restaurants, especially in Chinatown. I (11) ___Really do___ love Chinese food.

Chris: (12) ___I do too___. I've heard that the new Chinese restaurant on Grant Avenue is supposed to be really good.

Claire: (13) ___So have I___. Why don't we give it a try?

Chris: That sounds good. By the way, I have six cats. Do you like cats?

Claire: Well, (14) ___Kind of___.

Chris: That's O.K.—as long as you don't *hate* them. . . .

EXERCISE 6

One way to meet people is through personal ads in newspapers or magazines. These personal ads appeared in a local newspaper. Read them quickly and then read the statements that follow. Circle T (true) if you think the statement is true and F (false) if you think it is false.

(A) COULD THIS BE YOU?
You are attractive, slim, and athletic. You like dancing, eating candlelit dinners, and walking on the beach by moonlight. Like me, you also enjoy camping and hiking. You love dogs and you don't smoke. If you are the woman of my dreams, send a photo to Box 3092.

(B) BEAUTY & BRAINS
Warm, humorous, well-educated SF loves walking on the beach, dancing, cycling, and hiking. Seeks intelligent life partner with computer interests. P.S.—I'm allergic to cats, dogs, and smoking. Box 875.

(C) I'VE GOT YOU ON MY WAVELENGTH
Athletic, professional, DF, animal lover seeks active man who knows how to treat a lady. Box 4021.

(D) A FEW OF MY FAVORITE THINGS:
Cooking for my friends, cycling, walking on the beach with my dog, wise and witty women. I can't stand: snobs, cheap wine, jogging, people who smoke, women who wear makeup. DM looking for a special woman. Box 49.

---

1. A likes walking on the beach, and so do D and B.   T   F

2. B does not like smokers, and neither do A and C.   T   F

3. Cooking for friends is one of B's favorite pastimes.   T   F

4. D does not like women who wear a lot of makeup.   T   F

5. D likes dancing, and A does too.   T   F

6. A wants to find someone who likes hiking, and so does D.   T   F

7. Jogging and cycling are two of B's favorite sports.   T   F

Do you think any of these people would make a good couple? If so, why? If not, why not?

FOCUS 6 | Likes and Dislikes with Gerunds and Infinitives

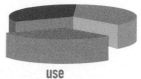

use

EXAMPLES	EXPLANATIONS
(a) **Cooking** is my favorite hobby. (b) I love **cooking.** Do you? (c) My favorite hobby is **cooking.**	*Gerunds* (nouns formed from verb + *-ing*) can be used as: the subject of a sentence the object of a sentence the complement of a sentence (something needed to complete the sentence)
(d) I like **to cook.** (e) I don't like **to swim.** (f) I hate **to go** to the dentist. (g) AWKWARD: **To cook** is my favorite hobby.	*Infinitives* (*to* + verb) are also used in talking about likes and dislikes. In this context, infinitives are usually used as objects of sentences or as complements, but they sound awkward as subjects.
(h) I don't like **swimming.** (i) I hate **going** to the dentist	When talking about likes and dislikes, you can usually use infinitives or gerunds. The verbs *hate, like,* and *love* can be followed by either a gerund or an infinitive.

EXERCISE 7

Look back at numbered list in Exercise 6.

1. Underline all the gerunds.
2. Check (✓) all the gerunds that are subjects and circle the gerunds that are objects or complements.
3. Replace the gerunds with infinitives where possible.
4. Rewrite sentences 2 and 4, using a gerund or an infinitive.

Sentence 2:

_____

_____

Sentence 4:

_____

_____

Use Your English

ACTIVITY 1 speaking

The purpose of this activity is to share information with one other person and then to report what you find to the rest of the class. While sharing information with your partner, try to find out **how many things you have in common.** Some ideas for starting your conversation are given below. When you have nothing more to say on this topic, decide on another one and find out what you have in common on that topic. Use the chart for your notes.

TOPIC	NOTES
family	Examples: any brothers and sisters?/grandparents alive?/father older than mother?

ACTIVITY 2 speaking

Form teams. Your job as a team is to find as many similarities as possible among the pairs of things listed below. The team that finds the most similarities is the winner.

You have to practice every day!

1. an apple and an orange

2. tennis and golf

3. hiking and jogging

4. learning a foreign language and learning to ride a bike

ACTIVITY 3 speaking

Form pairs or groups of three.

STEP 1 Think of fifteen to twenty statements using *so/too/either/neither.* Make sure they are meaningful. Write each statement on two cards, like this:

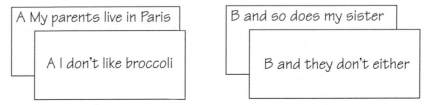

| A My parents live in Paris | B and so does my sister |
| A I don't like broccoli | B and they don't either |

Therefore, if you have twenty statements, you will have forty cards.

STEP 2 Get together with another pair or threesome. Place all the A cards in one pile and all the B cards in another pile. Shuffle each deck of cards carefully.

STEP 3 Put the A pile facedown on the table. Then distribute the B cards among the players. Do not look at the cards; place them facedown on the table in front of you.

STEP 4 The first player turns the first card from the A pile on the table and puts the first card from his or her B pile beside it. The player must not look at his or her card before putting it down on the table. The object of the game is to create meaningful sentences. If the two cards on the table do not make a meaningful match, the next player puts his or her B card down. The game continues in this way until a meaningful match is created. The first player to spot a match shouts "Match" to stop the game. If the match is acceptable, he or she collects all the B cards on the table. The next A card is then turned over and the game continues.

STEP 5 The player with the most cards at the end is the winner. This game should be played as quickly as possible.

ACTIVITY 4 writing

Who are you most similar to in your family? Write a description of your similarities and differences. If you wish, think of someone in your extended family—for example, a cousin, aunt, or grandparent.

ACTIVITY 5 speaking/listening

■ **STEP 1** Make a list of five popular musicians that you like or dislike. Or you can choose movies, movie stars, types of music, sports, writers, or books. Walk around the classroom and ask other students their opinions about your list. Find out how many students agree or disagree with you. Record your conversations or interviews.

■ **STEP 2** Make a report on your findings. Listen to the recording to make sure your report is accurate. Did your classmates use short phrases such as *I do too, so do I, I don't either, neither do I, sort of,* and *kind of*? If not, what did they use instead to agree and disagree with each other?

ACTIVITY 6 listening

■ **STEP 1** Listen to the audio of people talking about what they like and dislike. What general topic are they talking about? What specific topics do they mention?

CD Track 19 ■ **STEP 2** Number the statements below in the order that you hear them. Mark the first statement as number 1 and so forth.

_____ *I do too.* _____ *I don't either.* _____ *Sort of.*

_____ *So do I.* _____ *Neither do I.* _____ *Kind of.*

■ **STEP 3** Which statements do you agree and disagree with?

ACTIVITY 7 research on the web

InfoTrac® College Edition **Option:** Go to *InfoTrac* to look up a review of your favorite movie or music. Do you agree with the reviewer? Tell the class.

ACTIVITY 8 reflection

Work with a partner. Complete a chart like the one in the Opening Task on page 185 with things you both like and don't like about learning English. Then tell your class.

PRESENT PERFECT WITH *SINCE* AND *FOR*

UNIT GOALS

- Use present perfect to show a connection between past and present situations

- Form correct sentences with present perfect

- Know how to use *for* and *since* correctly

- Know which verbs not to use with present perfect

OPENING TASK

Personal Information

■ **STEP 1**

Look at the picture. Where are they? What are they talking about?

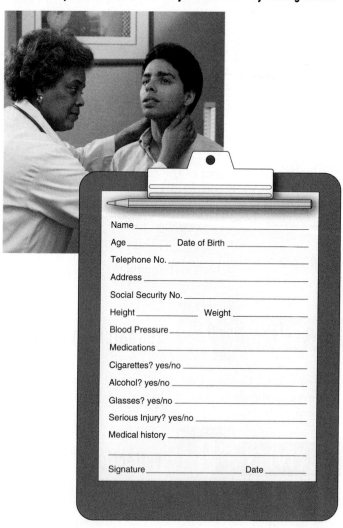

Name _____

Age _____ Date of Birth _____

Telephone No. _____

Address _____

Social Security No. _____

Height _____ Weight _____

Blood Pressure _____

Medications _____

Cigarettes? yes/no _____

Alcohol? yes/no _____

Glasses? yes/no _____

Serious Injury? yes/no _____

Medical history _____

_____

Signature _____ Date _____

STEP 2

Work in pairs. Student A, look at this page. Student B, look at page A-17.

Student A: Complete the information on the medical history form by asking your partner questions about Michael Menendez. Your partner will answer your questions by looking at pages A-16 and A-17. Use complete questions.

Example: Student A: *Does he smoke?*
Student B: *Yes, he does.*
Student A: *How long has he smoked?*

MEDICAL HISTORY					
Name	Michael Menendez				
Date of birth *08/24/75*	Cigarettes? Yes/No	Alcohol? <u>Yes</u>/No	Glasses? Yes/No	Serious Injuries? *Broken ankle*	Health Problems? _____
Height *5ft 11in* Weight _____	How long? _____ *Started* _____ *Stopped* _____	How much? *A glass of wine with dinner every night*	How long? Since _____	When? *In 1992*	How long? For _____

STEP 3

Use the information above to make sentences about Michael Menendez. Write complete sentences.

PAST:
1.
2.

PRESENT:
1.
2.

PAST AND PRESENT:
1.
2.

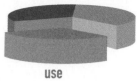
FOCUS 1 — Present Perfect: Connecting Past and Present

EXAMPLES	EXPLANATIONS
PAST (a) **I moved** to New York in 2002. (simple past)	Use the simple past for completed action in the past.
PRESENT (b) **I live** in New York now. (simple present)	Use the simple present for facts about present situations.
PAST AND PRESENT (c) **I have lived** in New York since 2002. (present perfect) (d) It is now 2006. **I have lived** in New York for four years. (present perfect)	Use the present perfect (*have* + past participle) to connect the past and present. One use of the present perfect is to tell us about something that began in the past and continues to the present. (For other uses of the present perfect, see Unit 14.)

EXERCISE 1

Use the information about Michael Menendez from the Opening Task on page 197 and page A-17 to complete the doctor's report below. Circle the simple present, simple past, or present perfect.

Medical Report on Michael Menendez

Michael Menendez spoke with me yesterday about serious headaches. He (1) has/had/has had these headaches for two months. His previous medical history is good. He (2) doesn't have/didn't have/hasn't had any serious illnesses. In 1992, he (3) is/was/has been in the hospital for three weeks, when he (4) breaks/broke/has broken his ankle in a skiing accident. He (5) doesn't smoke/didn't smoke/hasn't smoked: (6) he stops/stopped/has stopped six years ago, and he (7) doesn't smoke/didn't smoke/hasn't smoked since that time. He (8) wears /wore/has worn glasses when he reads and he (9) wears/wore/has worn them since 2003. He works/worked/has worked with computers since 1998. I examined Mr. Menendez and did several tests. I asked him to return next week.

Signed: Dr. Roberts

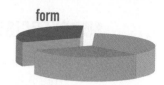

form

FOCUS 2 — Forming the Present Perfect

To form the present perfect use *have/has* + past participle.*

STATEMENT	NEGATIVE	QUESTION
I You We They } have gone. ('ve)	I You We They } have not gone. (haven't)	Have { I You We They } gone?
She He It } has gone. ('s)	She He It } has not gone. (hasn't)	Has { She He It } gone?

* See Appendix 5 on page A-13 for the past participles of some common irregular verbs.

EXERCISE 2

Write the questions that the doctor probably asked Mr. Menendez in order to get these responses.

Example: 1. _Do you drink?_ _____

Yes, a little. I drink a glass of wine with dinner every night.

2. _____

Yes, I do. I wear them when I read.

3. _____

I started wearing them in 1987.

4. _____

I've worn them since 1987.

5. _____

No, I don't smoke now.

6. _____

I stopped ten years ago.

7. _____

No, I haven't smoked since that time.

8. _____

Yes, I have had these headaches for two months.

EXERCISE 3

Work with a partner. Ask and answer questions about each other's medical history. Feel free to make up information on the following topics, or use the information about Michael Menendez on pages 197 and A-17 to answer questions.

Example: **A:** Have you had any serious illnesses?

B: Yes, I once had pneumonia when I was ten years old.

serious illnesses	time in hospital
smoking	drinking
eyesight	allergies
present health problem(s)	when problem(s) started

EXERCISE 4

Go back to Exercises 1 and 2. Look for the words *for* and *since*. In the boxes below, write down the word or words that directly follow *for* or *since*. The first example is *two months* with *for*, from Exercise 1.

SINCE	FOR
	two months

What does this tell you about the use of *since* and *for*? What kinds of words or phrases follow *since* and *for*?

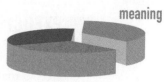

FOCUS 3   *For* and *Since*

EXAMPLES	EXPLANATIONS
(a) **for** two weeks (b) **for** ten years (c) **for** five minutes	*For* is used to show length of time (how long the period of time was).
(d) **since** 1985 (e) **since** my birthday (f) **since** I turned 40 (g) **since** Monday (h) **since** April	*Since* is used to show when a period of time began.

EXERCISE 5

What difference in meaning (if any) is there in each pair of statements? Discuss with a partner.

1. a. Anthony and Eva lived here for ten years.
   b. Anthony and Eva have lived here for ten years.

2. Anthony and Eva met in 1998.
   a. They have known each other for over ten years.
   b. They have known each other since 1998.

3. a. They have worked for the same company for a long time.
   b. They worked for the same company for a long time.

4. It is May. Eva started studying Italian three months ago.
   a. Eva has studied Italian for three months.
   b. Eva has studied Italian since February.

5. It is July.
   a. Anthony hasn't drunk any coffee for six months.
   b. Anthony stopped drinking coffee in January.

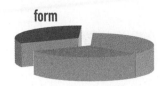

FOCUS 4 — *For* and *Since*

EXAMPLES	EXPLANATIONS
(a) She's worked here **(for)** several years.	The word *for* can be omitted in statements.
(b) **(For)** how long have you lived here?	*For* can also be omitted in questions.
(c) **Since** when have you lived here?	*Since* cannot be omitted. *"How long . . ."* is more common than *"Since when . . ."* in questions.
(d) NOT: When have you lived here?	
(e) I've lived here **since** January.	
(f) NOT: I've lived here January.	

EXERCISE 6

Look at the hotel register below. How many people are staying in the hotel right now? Who has stayed there the longest? Use the information from the register to make statements with the words given below.

Example: *Mr. and Mrs. Gordon stayed in the hotel for six nights.*

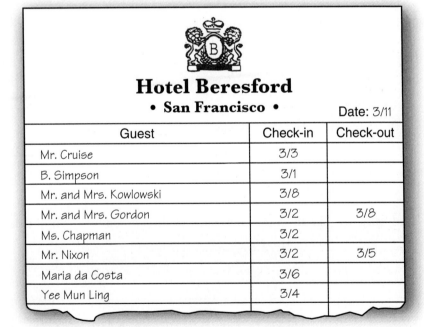

Hotel Beresford
• **San Francisco** •   Date: 3/11

Guest	Check-in	Check-out
Mr. Cruise	3/3	
B. Simpson	3/1	
Mr. and Mrs. Kowlowski	3/8	
Mr. and Mrs. Gordon	3/2	3/8
Ms. Chapman	3/2	
Mr. Nixon	3/2	3/5
Maria da Costa	3/6	
Yee Mun Ling	3/4	

1. Mr. and Mrs. Gordon/for
2. Maria da Costa/since
3. Yee Mun Ling/since
4. B. Simpson/for
5. Mr. and Mrs. Kowlowski/for
6. Ms. Chapman/since
7. Mr. Cruise/for
8. Mr. Nixon/for

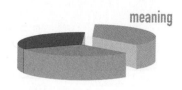

FOCUS 5 | Verbs Not Used with Present Perfect and *For*

EXAMPLES	EXPLANATIONS
(a) Shin **arrived** in the United States three years ago. (b) NOT: Shin has arrived in the United States for three years. (c) Shin **has lived** in the United States for three years.	Some verbs talk about an action that happens all at once, an action that doesn't continue for a period of time. In (c) we understand that it is the living in the United States that continues, not the arriving.
begin arrive meet *end leave stop*	For the same reason, these verbs are not usually used with present perfect and *for*.

EXERCISE 7

Rewrite these sentences. Be sure to use the present perfect and *since* or *for*.

Example: Karen wears glasses. She started to wear glasses when she was a child.
 Karen has worn glasses since she was a child.

1. He works for the TV station. He started working there eight years ago.

   _____

2. They are married. They got married in 1962.

   _____

3. She knows how to fix a car. She learned how to do it a long time ago.

   _____

4. Tom rides his bike to work. He started to do it when his car broke down.

   _____

5. I wanted to go to China several years ago. I still want to go now.

   _____

6. My brother started painting when he was in college, and he still paints now.

   _____

7. I was afraid of bats when I was a child, and I am afraid of them now.

   _____

8. My mother is in France. She went there last week.

   _____

9. My sister runs two miles every morning before breakfast. She started to do this when she was fifteen years old.

_____

10. They go to Cape Cod every summer. They started to do this twelve years ago.

_____

EXERCISE 8

Fill in the blanks with *since* or *for* OR the appropriate form of the verb in parentheses.

Leroy and Paula are having a party. Two of their guests, Lee and Bob, have just met.

Lee: (1) _____ Have you known Leroy and Paula (2) _____

a long time?

Bob: I (3) _____ (know) Paula

(4) _____ my senior year in college. I first

(5) _____ (meet) Leroy at their wedding two years ago.

What about you?

Lee: I'm a colleague of Leroy's. We (6) _____ (work) together

(7) _____ several years.

Bob: Oh, Leroy (8) _____ (show) me some of your work last week.

It's great.

Lee: Thanks. What do you do?

Bob: I (9) _____ (teach) French (10) _____ ten years,

but I (11) _____ (quit) a couple of years ago. Now I'm an actor.

Lee: An actor! I thought you looked familiar.

Bob: Well, not really. I (12) _____ (not work) as an actor

(13) _____ last October. In fact, last night I

(14) _____ (start) to work as a waiter at the Zenon.

Lee: Really? I (15) _____ (eat) there last night. *That's*

why you look familiar!

EXERCISE 9

Look for mistakes in the following passage. Correct any mistakes that you find. One mistake has been corrected for you.

1. My sister is very good at languages. She studies

2. Italian at the language institute. She started studying

3. Italian in 1993, so she ~~studies~~ *has studied* Italian several years. When

4. she was a child, she wanted to learn Russian and she still

5. wants to learn it. She has wanted to learn Russian

6. since a long time, but Russian courses are not offered

7. at the language schools near her home. Two years ago

8. she has found out that the local community college offers

9. courses in Chinese, so she started learning Chinese.

10. Unfortunately, she doesn't have a car, so she takes the bus

11. to school since two years.

Use Your English

ACTIVITY **1** speaking

Work in pairs or groups of three. Complete the following with information about your partner(s). Make a list of appropriate questions and then ask your partner(s) the questions. Here are some sample questions:

How long have you studied English?   *How long have you lived in this town?*

1. _____ for _____ hours.

2. _____ since _____.

3. _____ for _____.

4. _____ for _____ years.

5. _____ since _____.

ACTIVITY 2 speaking

Work individually. Respond to this survey. Each response is a number.

——— The number of people you have talked to today

——— The number of weeks, months, or years you have known your oldest friend

——— The number of weeks, months, or years you have studied in this school

——— The number of hours or minutes since you last ate something

——— The number of minutes you have been in this classroom

Work in pairs. Say one number to your partner (in random order). Your partner has to guess what each number means.

Example:
A: *Five*
B: *Is that the number of weeks you have studied in this school?*

ACTIVITY 3 speaking/listening

■ **STEP 1** Work with a partner. Read the statements in the chart on page 208 and try to match each statement to someone in your class. Write the name in the column marked Guesses.

■ **STEP 2** Next, ask your classmates questions using *How long have you . . . ?* in order to find out who has done each thing the longest and shortest amounts of time. Fill in the answers in the column marked Facts.

Continued on the next page

ACTIVITY 3 continued

GUESSES	WHO.	FACTS
_____	has studied English the longest time?	_____
_____	has been married the longest time?	_____
_____	has owned his or her watch the longest time?	_____
_____	has known how to drive the longest time?	_____
_____	has known how to drive the shortest time?	_____
_____	has had the shoes he or she is wearing today the longest time?	_____
_____	has worn glasses the longest time?	_____
_____	has worn glasses the shortest time?	_____
_____	has had the same hair style the longest time?	_____

ACTIVITY 4 speaking/listening/writing

In this activity, you will find out how different countries are governed.

■ **STEP 1** Get together with a group of classmates from different countries, if possible. First use the three charts on page 209 to note and list information about your own country or another country you are familiar with. We have done some for you, as examples.

■ **STEP 2** When you have all filled in the charts, begin sharing your information. Then use the charts to take more notes on what your classmates tell you. In the first two charts, check (✓) the appropriate box or write in the box marked other. In the third chart, write notes.

■ **STEP 3** Be ready to share this information with the rest of the class.

COUNTRY	TYPE OF LEADERSHIP				
	President	Monarch*	Prime minister	Military	Other
Great Britain		✓	✓		

* King, queen, emperor, etc.

COUNTRY	HOW CURRENT LEADER CAME INTO POWER				
	Election	Succession*	Coup**	Other	
Great Britain	✓ (Prime Minister)	✓ (Queen)			

* *Succession:* the act of a position or title passing from one person to another, usually a relative
** *Coup*: a sudden or violent seizure of power by a group that has not been elected

COUNTRY	WHAT CURRENT LEADER HAS DONE		
	Length of time the current leader has been in power	Best thing he or she has done while in power	Worst thing he or she has done while in power***

*** Talk about the leader of your country or another country for which you've listed information in the blank

CD Track 20

■ **STEP 1**

You are going to hear a job interview with a man applying for a job as an office manager. Listen to the job interview carefully. Do you think the man will get the job? Why or why not? Discuss with a partner.

■ **STEP 2**

Match the first part of each sentence in column A with the second part in column B.

A	B
1. I've worked	a. being part of a team.
2. I've been	b. able to solve every problem.
3. I've enjoyed	c. there for about three years.
4. I have found out	d. in charge of training the new staff.
5. I've learned	e. more or less everything there is to know about the job.
6. I haven't always been	f. how to work with people.

■ **STEP 3**

Listen to the audio again. This time, listen to all the interviewer's questions. Write them in the chart.

INTERVIEWER'S QUESTIONS
1.
2.
3.
4.
5.
6.

■ **STEP 4**

Role-play the interview with a partner. Change any of the questions or answers if you want.

ACTIVITY 6 — speaking/listening

STEP 1   Find a classmate, a friend, or an acquaintance who is studying the same field as you, or who has or wants a job like yours. Conduct a practice job interview. You can work together to come up with questions, which should include when things happened and for how long: work experience, job history, and education. Feel free to make up information!

STEP 2   Decide who will be the "employer" (the interviewer) and who will be the "employee" (the interviewee). Take turns if there is time. Record the interviews.

STEP 3   Listen to the recording. Write down all the sentences with the present perfect. In each case, was it used correctly? Were *since* and *for* used? Were there cases where the present perfect should have been used but wasn't?

ACTIVITY 7 — research on the web/writing

STEP 1   Choose a country that you are interested in. Go on the Internet and use a search engine such as Google® or Yahoo® to find out about the political system in that country. What kind of government does it have? When and how did the current leader come into power? What has the current leader done while he or she has been in power?

STEP 2   Write a brief summary of the information you found. Exchange reports with a classmate and check to make sure that the present perfect was used correctly.

ACTIVITY 8 — reflection

Write three things you have done that have helped you to learn English. Make a class list and display the results as a class poster.

APPENDICES

APPENDIX 1   Forming Verb Tenses

Appendix 1A   Simple Present (verb/verb + –s)

Statement	Negative	Question	Short Answers
I You We They } work.	I You We They } do not/ don't work.	Does { I you we they } work?	Yes, { I you we they } do.
He She It } works.	He She It } does not/ doesn't work.	Does { he she it } work?	Yes, { he she it } does.
			No, { I you we they } don't.
			No, { he she it } doesn't.

Appendix 1B   PRESENT PROGESSIVE (*am/is/are* + verb + *–ing*)

Statement	Negative	Question	Short Answers
I am (I'm) working.	I am not (I'm not) working.	Am I working?	Yes, I am. No, I'm not.
You are (you're) working.	You are not (aren't) working.	Are you working?	Yes, you are. No, you aren't. OR You're not.
She/He/It is (She's/He's/It's) working.	She/He/It is not (isn't) working.	Is she/he/it working?	Yes, she/he/it is. No, she/he/it isn't. OR She's/He's/It's not.
We are (We're) working.	We are not (aren't) working.	Are we working?	Yes, we are. No, we aren't. OR We're not.
They are (They're) working.	They are not (aren't) working.	Are they working?	Yes, they are. No, they aren't. OR They're not.

Appendix 1C   Simple Past (verb + *–ed* or irregular form)

Statement	Negative	Question	Short Answers
I You We They } worked. He She It	I You We They } did not/ didn't work. He She It	Did { I you we they work? he she it	Yes, { I you we they did. he she it No, { I you we they didn't he she it

Appendix 1D   Past Progressive (*was/ were* + verb + *–ing*)

Statement	Negative	Question	Short Answers
I She } was sleeping. He It	I She } was not sleeping. He (wasn't) It	Was { I she sleeping? he it	Yes, { I she } was. he it
We You } were sleeping. They	We You } were not sleeping. They (weren't)	Were { we You sleeping? they	No, { we You } weren't. they

Appendix 1E — Present Perfect (*has/have* + verb + past participle)

Statement	Negative	Question	Short Answers
I / You / We / They — have gone. ('ve)	I / You / We / They — have not gone. (haven't)	Have — I / you / we / they — gone?	Yes, — I / you / we / they — have.
She / He / It — has gone. ('s)	She / He / It — has not gone. (hasn't)	Has — she / he / it — gone?	Yes, — he / she / it — has.
			No, — I / you / we / they — haven't.
			No, — he / she / it — hasn't.

Appendix 1F — Present Perfect Progressive (*has/have* + *been* + verb + *–ing*)

Statement	Negative	Question	Short Answers
I / You / We / They — have been ('ve) sleeping.	I / You / We / They — have not been (haven't) sleeping.	Have — I / you / we / they — been sleeping?	Yes, — I / you / we / they — have been.
She / He / It — has been ('s) sleeping.	She / He / It — has not been (hasn't) sleeping.	Has — she / he / it — been sleeping?	Yes, — he / she / it — has been.
			No, — I / you / we / they — haven't been.
			No, — he / she / it — hasn't been.

Appendix 1G Past Perfect (*had* + verb + past participle)

Statement	Negative	Question	Short Answers
I You We They She He It } had ('d) arrived.	I You We They She He It } had not (hadn't) arrived.	Had { I you we they she he it } arrived?	Yes, { I you we they he she it } had. No, { I you we they he she it } hadn't.

Appendix 1H Future: *will* (*will* + verb)

Statement	Negative	Question	Short Answers
I You We They She He It } will leave. ('ll).	I You We They She He It } will not (won't) leave.	Will { I you we they she he it } leave?	Yes, { I you we they he she it } will. No, { I you we they he she it } won't.

Appendix 1I Future: *be going to* (am/is/are + verb)

Statement	Negative	Question	Short Answers
I am going to leave. ('m)	I am not going to leave. ('m)	Am I going to leave?	Yes, I am.
You / We / They } are going ('re) to leave.	You / We / They } are not going (aren't) to leave.	Are you / we / they } going to leave?	Yes, you / we / they } are.
She / He / It } is going ('s) to leave.	She / He / It } is not going (isn't) to leave.	Is she / He / it }	Yes, he / She / it } is.
			No, I am not. ('m not.)
			No, you / we / they } are not. (aren't)
			No, he / she / it } is not. (isn't)

APPENDIX 2   Forming the Passive

Appendix 2A   The *Be* Passive

To form the passive, use the appropriate tense of *be*, follwed by the past participle (pp).

	Tense	Form of *Be*	
(a) Wool **is produced** here.	Simple Present	*am/is/are*	+ pp
(b) Wool **is being produced** here right now.	Present Progressive	*am/is/are being*	+ pp
(c) Wool **was produced** here.	Simple Past	*was/were*	+ pp
(d) Wool **was** being produced here ten years ago.	Past Progressive	*was/were being*	+ pp
(e) Wool **has been produced** here since 1900.	Present Perfect	*have/has been*	+ pp
(f) Wool **had been produced** here when the island was discovered.	Past Perfect	*had been*	+ pp
(g) Wool **will be produced** here next year.	Future (*will*)	*will be*	+ pp
(h) Wool **is going to be produced** here.	Future (*be going to*)	*am/is/are going to be*	+ pp
(i) Wool **will have been produced** here by the year 2010.	Future Perfect	*will have been*	+ pp

Appendix 2B   The *Get* Passive

	Tense	Form of *Get*	
(a) Her cookies always **get eaten**.	Simple Present	*get/gets*	+ pp
(b) Her cookies **are getting eaten**.	Persent Progressive	*am/is/are getting*	+ pp
(c) Her cookies **got eaten**.	Simple Past	*got*	+ pp
(d) Her cookies **were getting eaten**.	Past Progressive	*was/were getting*	+ pp
(e) Her cookies **have gotten eaten**.	Present Perfect	*have/has gotten*	+ pp
(f) Her cookies **had gotten eaten**.	Past Perfect	*had gotten*	+ pp
(g) Her cookies **will be eaten**.	Future (*will*)	*will get*	+ pp
(h) Her cookies **are going to get eaten**.	Future (*be going to*)	*am/is/are going to get*	+ pp
(i) Her cookies **will have gotten eaten** by the time we get home.	Future Perfect	*will have gotten*	+ pp

APPENDIX 3   Forming Conditionals

Appendix 3A   Factual Conditionals

If Clause	Main Clause
[*If* + simple present] If you heat water,	[simple present] it boils.

Appendix 3B   Future Conditionals

If Clause	Main Clause
[*If* + simple present] If you study hard,	[*will/be going to* + base verb] you will get a good grade.

Appendix 3C   Hypothetical Conditionals

If Clause	Main Clause
[*If* + simple past] (a) If we had lots of money, [*If* + Be very → subjunctive *were*] (b) If I were rich,	[*would* (*'d*) + base verb] we'd travel around the world. [*would* + base verb] I'd travel around the world.

Appendix 3D Past Hypothetical Conditionals

If Clause	Main Clause
[*If* + past perfect] If you had called me,	[*would* + *have* (*'ve*) + *verb* + past participle] I would have come to see you

APPENDIX 4   Overview of Modal Auxilliaries

Appendix 4A   Probability and Possibility (Unit 5)

Possible (less than 50% certain)	Probable (about 90% certain)	Certain (100% certain)
less certain ↕ He *could* play golf. He *might* play golf. He *may* play golf. **more certain**	He *must* play golf.	He plays golf.
less certain ↕ She *could* be a doctor. She *might* be doctor. She *may* be a doctor. **more certain**	She *must* be a doctor.	She is a doctor.
less certain ↕ *Could* he play golf? *Might* he play golf? **more certain**	—	*Does* he play golf?
less certain ↕ *Could* she be a doctor? *Might* she be a doctor? **more certain**	—	*Is* she a doctor?
less certain ↕ He *might not* play golf. He *may not* play golf. He *couldn't* play golf. **more certain**	He *must not* play golf.	He *does not/doesn't* play golf.
less certain ↕ She *might not* be a doctor. She *may not* be a doctor. She *couldn't/can't* be a doctor. **more certain**	She *must not* be a doctor.	She *is not/isn't* a doctor.

Present Forms

Question Forms

Negative Forms

Continued on next page

Continued from previous page

Possible (less than 50% certain)	Probable (about 90% certain)	Certain (100% certain)
less certain He *could have* played golf. He *might have* played golf. He *may have* played golf. **more certain**	He *must have* played golf.	He played golf.
less certain She *could have* been a doctor. She *might have* been a doctor. She *may have* been a doctor. **more certain**	She *must have* been a doctor.	She *was* a doctor.
less certain *Could* he *have* played golf? *Might* he *have* played golf? **more certain**	—	*Did* he play golf?
less certain *Could* she *have* been a doctor? *Might* she *have* been a doctor? **more certain**	—	*Was* she a doctor?
less certain He *could be* playing golf. He *might be* playing golf. He *may be* playing golf. **more certain**	He *must be* playing golf.	He *is* playing golf.
less certain He *could have been* playing golf. He *might have been* playing golf. He *may have been* playing golf. **more certain**	He *must have been* playing golf.	He *was* playing golf./ He *has* been playing golf.
less certain It *could* rain tomorrow. It *may (not)* rain tomorrow. It *might (not)* rain tomorrow. **more certain**	It *will probably* rain tomorrow. It *probably won't* rain tomorrow.	It *will/will/not/won't* rain tomorrow.

Past Forms (rows 1–4)
Progressive Forms (rows 5–6)
Future Forms (row 7)

Appendix 4B   Giving Advice and Expressing Opinions (Unit 10)

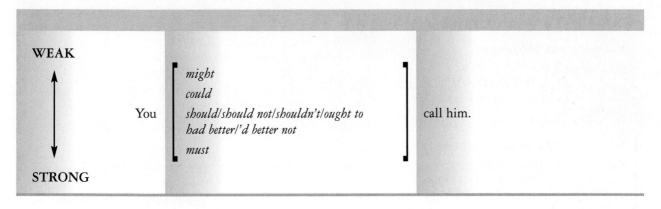

WEAK

↕

STRONG

You
- might
- could
- should/should not/shouldn't/ought to
- had better/'d better not
- must

call him.

Appendix 4C   Necessity and Obligation (Unit 11)

PRESENT	PAST	FUTURE
Necessary and Obligatory		
She *must* go.	—	She *must* go.
She's/*has got to* go.	—	She's/*has got to* go.
She *has to* go.	She *had to* go.	She *has to* go./ She'll/*will have to* go.
Not Necessary and not Obligatory		
She *doesn't/does not have to* go.	She *didn't/did not have to* go.	She *doesn't/does not have to* go. She *won't/will not have to* go.

Appendix 4D   Probihition and Permission (Unit 11)

PRESENT	PAST	FUTURE
Prohibited and not Permitted		
We *can't/cannot* smoke in here.	We *couldn't/could not* smoke in here.	We *will not/won't be able to* smoke in here.
We *mustn't/must not* smoke in here.	—	
Permitted		
We *can* smoke in here.	We *could* smoke in here.	We *will be able to* smoke in here.

BASE FORM	PAST-TENSE FORM	PAST PARTICIPLE	BASE FORM	PAST-TENSE FORM	PAST PARTICIPLE
be	was	been	leave	left	left
become	became	become	lend	lent	lent
begin	began	begun	let	let	let
bend	bent	bent	lose	lost	lost
bite	bit	bitten	make	made	made
blow	blew	blown	meet	met	met
break	broke	broken	pay	paid	paid
bring	brought	brought	put	put	put
build	built	built	quit	quit	quit
buy	bought	bought	read	read*	read
catch	caught	caught	ride	rode	ridden
choose	chose	chosen	ring	rang	rung
come	came	come	run	ran	run
cost	cost	cost	say	said	said
cut	cut	cut	see	saw	seen
dig	dug	dug	sell	sold	sold
do	did	done	send	sent	sent
draw	drew	drawn	shake	shook	shaken
drink	drank	drunk	shoot	shot	shot
drive	drove	driven	shut	shut	shut
eat	ate	eaten	sing	sang	sung
fall	fell	fallen	sit	sat	sat
feed	fed	fed	sleep	slept	slept
feel	felt	felt	speak	spoke	spoken
fight	fought	fought	spend	spent	spent
find	found	found	stand	stood	stood
fly	flew	flown	steal	stole	stolen
forget	forgot	forgotten	swim	swam	swum
get	got	gotten	take	took	taken
give	gave	given	teach	taught	taught
go	went	gone	tear	tore	torn
grow	grew	grown	tell	told	told
hang	hung	hung	think	thought	thought
have	had	had	throw	threw	thrown
hear	heard	heard	understand	understood	understood
hide	hid	hidden	wake	woke	woken
hit	hit	hit	wear	wore	worn
hold	held	held	win	won	won
hurt	hurt	hurt	write	wrote	written
keep	kept	kept			
know	knew	known			
lead	led	led			

* Pronounce the base form: /rid/; pronounce the past-tense form: /red/.

ANSWER KEY
(for puzzles and problems only)

UNIT 1

Answers to Exercise 10 (page 12)

- Horses sleep standing up.
- Bats use their ears to "see."
- Scorpions have twelve eyes.
- Elephants sometimes go for four days without water.

- Swans stay with the same mates all their lives.
- Antelopes run at 70 miles per hour.
- Bears sleep during the winter months.
- Spiders live for about two years.

UNIT 2

Student B Opening Task (page 18)

Picture B

Answers to Exercise 5 (page 25)

1. (example) See you later
2. I hear you
3. Know what I mean?
4. I love you
5. I don't think so
6. I don't know
7. Believe it or not
8. You are (You're) welcome

UNIT 4

Answers to Exercise 10 (page 62)

1.	A	5.	M	9.	E	13.	O	17.	K
2.	P	6.	R	10.	B	14.	F	18.	D
3.	G	7.	Q	11.	I	15.	C	19.	S
4.	J	8.	N	12.	L	16.	H		

UNIT 5

"Official" Answers to Activity 1 (page 84)

1. A giraffe passing a window.   2. A pencil seen from the end.   3. A cat climbing a tree.

UNIT 6

Solution to the Opening Task (pages 88–89)

Mrs. Meyer killed her husband. She entered the bathroom while he was brushing his teeth, and she hit him over the head with the bathroom scale. Then she turned on the shower and put the soap on the floor. *How do we know this?*

- From the toothbrush: He was brushing his teeth, not walking out of the shower.
- From the footprints: The shoe prints indicate a woman's high heeled shoes leading from the shower.
- From the bathroom scale: The scale does not indicate zero.

Pair Work Task: Activity 1 (page 99)

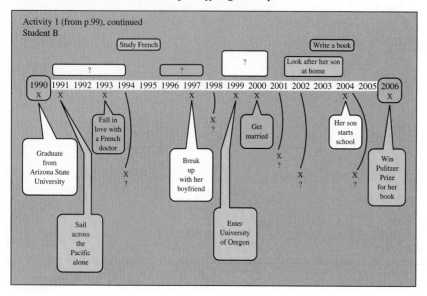

UNIT 7

Solution to the Opening Task (pages 104–105)

Linda	Bob	George
Susan	**Diana**	Frank
	Carla	

UNIT 9

Solution to Opening Task (page 137)

a. 2, b. 1, c. 4, d. 3

MEDICAL HISTORY					
Name	*Micheal Menendez*				
Date of birth _/_/ 75	Cigarettes? Yes/No	Alcohol Yes/No	Glasses? Yes/No	Serious Injuries? _____	Health problems? *Headaches*
Height _____ Weight 185 lbs	How long? *For 5 years* *Started <u>1995</u>* *Stopped <u>2000</u>*	How much?	How long? *Since <u>2003</u>*	When? *In _____*	How long? *For 2 months*

UNIT 10

Solution to Exercise 7 (page 159)

First, the woman should take the mouse to the car, leaving the cat with the cheese. Next, she should return and pick up the cat and take it to the car. As soon as she gets to the car with the cat, she should remove the mouse and take it with her, leaving the cat in the car. When she gets back to the shopping area, she should pick up the cheese and leave the mouse. Then she should take the cheese to the car and leave it there with the cat. Finally, she should return to collect the mouse and bring it with her to the car.

UNIT 13

Student B Opening Task (page 197)

Student B: Complete the information on the medical history form by asking your partner questions about Michael Menendez. Your partner will answer your questions by looking at page 197. Use complete questions.

Example: Student A: *Does he smoke?*
              Student B: *Yes, he does.*
              Student A: *How long has he smoked?*

UNIT 22

Student B Solution to Exercise 4 (page 317)

Picture B

UNIT 23

Student B Opening Task (page 329)

UNIT 24

Solution to the Opening Task (page 349)

The person _who_ loves Lee is _Sid_. The person _who_ loves Kit is _Tracy_.
The person _whom_ Sid loves is _Lee_. The person _whom_ Tracy loves is _Kit._

Unit 25

Opening Task (page 364) Possible answers

- If I had a knife, I would use it to cut wood for a fire.
- If I saw a ship, I would try to make a fire so they would see the smoke.
- If I found human footprints, I would follow them to find out who it was.
- If I didn't have any water, I would get juice from fruit or plants.
- If I met another survivor, I would work with him or her to make a plan / escape / build a shelter / get help.

CREDITS

Text Credits

p. 88: From *Crime and Puzzlement* by Lawrence Treat, Illustration by Leslie Cabarga. Reprinted by permission of David R. Gordine, Publisher Inc. Copyright 1981 by Lawrence Treat, Illustrations by Leslie Cabarga.

p. 176: Adapted with permission from "How not to collide with local road laws," *The European* (Magazine section) June 9, 1985.

p. 298: Adapted with permission from "Volunteers Head South to Help Victims of Hurricane Katrina" *Los Angeles Business Journal*, Sept 12, 2005 v27 i37 p.10(1).

p. 306: Adapted with permission from "Burma: A Travel Survival Kit" by Tony Wheeler. Lonely Planet Publications 1982.

Photo Credits

Page 0: Top: © Photos.com/RF, Bottom: © Photos.com/RF
Page 5: Top Left: © ImageState/Alamy, Bottom Left: © Design Pics Inc./Alamy/RF, Top Right: ©Henning von Holleben/Photonica/Getty, Bottom Right: © Erik Dreyer/Stone/Getty
Page 11: Photos.com/RF
Page 15: © Stockbyte Platinum/Alamy/RF
Page 18: © Photos.com/RF
Page 25: © Nick Koudis/Photodisc Red/Getty/RF
Page 34: © A. Inden/zefa/Corbis
Page 43: © IndexOpen/RF
Page 48: © Julia Fullerton-Batten/Stone+/Getty
Page 49: © Photos.com/RF
Page 59: © BananaStock /Alamy/RF
Page 62: Left: © Jon Feingersh/zefa/Corbis, Right: © Rick Gomez/Corbis
Page 70: © Photos.com/RF
Page 76: © Marsi/Photodisc Red/Getty/RF
Page 86: Left: © Andrew Holt /Alamy, Left Center: © Charles Gullung/Photonica/Getty, Right Center: © Comstock Premium / Alamy/RF, Right: © NASA / Photo Researchers, Inc
Page 96: © Getty Images
Page 98: © Charlotte Thege / Peter Arnold, Inc.
Page 99: © Photos.com/RF

INDEX

beliefs (*See* opinions and beliefs)
believe, 26
belong, 26
best, 295
break down, 341
by
    passive verbs using, 318–319
    past perfect tense using, 277–278
by the time, past perfect tense using, 277–278

C

call off, 333
can/could, 248–256
    permission expressed using, 168
    requests using, 256
cannot/can't
    used to express probability, 72–73
    used to express prohibition, 168, 173–174
catch on, 341
certainly, 190
certainty about a situation expressed using
    modals, 72–73
choice questions, 58–59
clauses, *as...as* and *not as...as* used with, 110
clean up, 335
come across, 337
come back, 341
come to, 341
comma
    after clause with *before* or *after*, 277
    used with dependent clauses, 94–98
comparatives, 104–119 (*See also* similarities and differences)
conditionals, 362–381
    factual, 375
    future, 371–372
    future *vs.* hypothetical, 373–374
    hypothetical, 364–365
    if clauses used in, 364–377
    may used in, 376–377
    might used in, 376–377
    past hypothetical, 367–370
    past perfect tense and
    will used in, 376–377
    word order for, 366–367
    would used as, 376–377
connecting events, present perfect tense to express, 278–279
containers for food, 122
continuing actions, *still* to express, 262–271
contrast, past perfect tense to express, 278–279
cost, 26
could, 72, 81, 248–256
    advice expressed using, 157–160
    in permissions, 255
    in polite requests, 250
    requests using, 256
could not/couldn't used to express prohibition, 186

couldn't/can't, 72–63
count nouns
    articles used with, 286–298
    degree complements using, 142
    measure words and, 125–128
    quantifiers and, 129–130
    some used with, 286, 290
couple, 130

D

decisions, *will* when making, 41–43
definite articles, 286–287
degree complements, 136–149
    count nouns and, 142
    enough used with adjective/adverb + infinitive, 140
    enough used with noun/verb + infinitive, 140
    enough/not enough as, 138–141
    noncount nouns and, 142
    too as, 138–141
    too little/too few as, 142–143
    too much/too many as, 142–143
    too placed before adjectives/adverbs, 140
    too vs. very in, 143–145
dependent clauses
    comma used with, 94–98
    time clauses as, 94–98
differences (*See* similarities and differences)
dislike, 26
dislikes (*See* likes and dislikes)
do
    as...as and *not as...as* used with, 110
    emphatic, 190–191
do not have to
    future tense and, 178–180
    lack of necessity expressed using, 175–177
    past tense and, 178–180
    permission expressed using, 168
    present tense and, 178–180
do you mind
    permissions expressed using, 255
    requests using, 256
do you want used in making offers, 238–247

E

eat out, 341
–ed to form participles, 355–358
either used to express similarity in likes and dislikes, 186
emotions and feelings, nonprogressive or stative verbs to
    describe, 26
emphatic *do*, 190–191
enough
    as degree complement, 138–141
    used with adjective/adverb + infinitive, 140
    used with noun/verb + infinitive, 140
ever used in questions, 217
everyone, 129